ISBN 0-8373-0456-3

C-456   CAREER EXAMINATION SERIES

This is your
PASSBOOK® for...

Airport
Security
Guard

Test Preparation Study Guide

Questions & Answers

NATIONAL LEARNING CORPORATION

34.95

Copyright © 2015 by

National Learning Corporation

212 Michael Drive, Syosset, New York 11791

(516) 921-8888
(800) 645-6337
FAX: (516) 921-8743
www.passbooks.com
sales @ passbooks.com
info @ passbooks.com

PRINTED IN THE UNITED STATES OF AMERICA

PASSBOOK®

NOTICE

PASSBOOK® SERIES

THE *PASSBOOK® SERIES* has been created to prepare applicants and candidates for the ultimate academic battlefield — the examination room.

At some time in our lives, each and every one of us may be required to take an examination — for validation, matriculation, admission, qualification, registration, certification, or licensure.

Based on the assumption that every applicant or candidate has met the basic formal educational standards, has taken the required number of courses, and read the necessary texts, the *PASSBOOK® SERIES* furnishes the one special preparation which may assure passing with confidence, instead of failing with insecurity. Examination questions — together with answers — are furnished as the basic vehicle for study so that the mysteries of the examination and its compounding difficulties may be eliminated or diminished by a sure method.

This book is meant to help you pass your examination provided that you qualify and are serious in your objective.

The entire field is reviewed through the huge store of content information which is succinctly presented through a provocative and challenging approach — the question-and-answer method.

A climate of success is established by furnishing the correct answers at the end of each test.

You soon learn to recognize types of questions, forms of questions, and patterns of questioning. You may even begin to anticipate expected outcomes.

You perceive that many questions are repeated or adapted so that you can gain acute insights, which may enable you to score many sure points.

You learn how to confront new questions, or types of questions, and to attack them confidently and work out the correct answers.

You note objectives and emphases, and recognize pitfalls and dangers, so that you may make positive educational adjustments.

Moreover, you are kept fully informed in relation to new concepts, methods, practices, and directions in the field.

You discover that you are actually taking the examination all the time: you are preparing for the examination by "taking" an examination, not by reading extraneous and/or supererogatory textbooks.

In short, this PASSBOOK®, used directedly, should be an important factor in helping you to pass your test.

AIRPORT SECURITY GUARD

DUTIES
Under direct supervision, an employee in this class patrols airport grounds on foot or by car, and responds to requests for assistance to insure passenger and airport security. Work involves considerable public contact in the daily performance of duties. Supervision is received from a technical or administrative supervisor through observation of work and conferences. Does related work as required.

SCOPE OF THE EXAMINATION
The multiple-choice written test will cover knowledge, skills, and/or abilities in such areas as:
1. Applying written information in a safety and security setting;
2. Following directions (maps);
3. Preparing written material; and
4. Understanding and interpreting written material.

———

HOW TO TAKE A TEST

I. YOU MUST PASS AN EXAMINATION

A. *WHAT EVERY CANDIDATE SHOULD KNOW*

Examination applicants often ask us for help in preparing for the written test. What can I study in advance? What kinds of questions will be asked? How will the test be given? How will the papers be graded?

As an applicant for a civil service examination, you may be wondering about some of these things. Our purpose here is to suggest effective methods of advance study and to describe civil service examinations.

Your chances for success on this examination can be increased if you know how to prepare. Those "pre-examination jitters" can be reduced if you know what to expect. You can even experience an adventure in good citizenship if you know why civil service exams are given.

B. *WHY ARE CIVIL SERVICE EXAMINATIONS GIVEN?*

Civil service examinations are important to you in two ways. As a citizen, you want public jobs filled by employees who know how to do their work. As a job seeker, you want a fair chance to compete for that job on an equal footing with other candidates. The best-known means of accomplishing this two-fold goal is the competitive examination.

Exams are widely publicized throughout the nation. They may be administered for jobs in federal, state, city, municipal, town or village governments or agencies.

Any citizen may apply, with some limitations, such as the age or residence of applicants. Your experience and education may be reviewed to see whether you meet the requirements for the particular examination. When these requirements exist, they are reasonable and applied consistently to all applicants. Thus, a competitive examination may cause you some uneasiness now, but it is your privilege and safeguard.

C. *HOW ARE CIVIL SERVICE EXAMS DEVELOPED?*

Examinations are carefully written by trained technicians who are specialists in the field known as "psychological measurement," in consultation with recognized authorities in the field of work that the test will cover. These experts recommend the subject matter areas or skills to be tested; only those knowledges or skills important to your success on the job are included. The most reliable books and source materials available are used as references. Together, the experts and technicians judge the difficulty level of the questions.

Test technicians know how to phrase questions so that the problem is clearly stated. Their ethics do not permit "trick" or "catch" questions. Questions may have been tried out on sample groups, or subjected to statistical analysis, to determine their usefulness.

Written tests are often used in combination with performance tests, ratings of training and experience, and oral interviews. All of these measures combine to form the best-known means of finding the right person for the right job.

II. HOW TO PASS THE WRITTEN TEST

A. NATURE OF THE EXAMINATION

To prepare intelligently for civil service examinations, you should know how they differ from school examinations you have taken. In school you were assigned certain definite pages to read or subjects to cover. The examination questions were quite detailed and usually emphasized memory. Civil service exams, on the other hand, try to discover your present ability to perform the duties of a position, plus your potentiality to learn these duties. In other words, a civil service exam attempts to predict how successful you will be. Questions cover such a broad area that they cannot be as minute and detailed as school exam questions.

In the public service similar kinds of work, or positions, are grouped together in one "class." This process is known as *position-classification*. All the positions in a class are paid according to the salary range for that class. One class title covers all of these positions, and they are all tested by the same examination.

B. FOUR BASIC STEPS

1) Study the announcement

How, then, can you know what subjects to study? Our best answer is: "Learn as much as possible about the class of positions for which you've applied." The exam will test the knowledge, skills and abilities needed to do the work.

Your most valuable source of information about the position you want is the official exam announcement. This announcement lists the training and experience qualifications. Check these standards and apply only if you come reasonably close to meeting them.

The brief description of the position in the examination announcement offers some clues to the subjects which will be tested. Think about the job itself. Review the duties in your mind. Can you perform them, or are there some in which you are rusty? Fill in the blank spots in your preparation.

Many jurisdictions preview the written test in the exam announcement by including a section called "Knowledge and Abilities Required," "Scope of the Examination," or some similar heading. Here you will find out specifically what fields will be tested.

2) Review your own background

Once you learn in general what the position is all about, and what you need to know to do the work, ask yourself which subjects you already know fairly well and which need improvement. You may wonder whether to concentrate on improving your strong areas or on building some background in your fields of weakness. When the announcement has specified "some knowledge" or "considerable knowledge," or has used adjectives like "beginning principles of…" or "advanced … methods," you can get a clue as to the number and difficulty of questions to be asked in any given field. More questions, and hence broader coverage, would be included for those subjects which are more important in the work. Now weigh your strengths and weaknesses against the job requirements and prepare accordingly.

3) Determine the level of the position

Another way to tell how intensively you should prepare is to understand the level of the job for which you are applying. Is it the entering level? In other words, is this the position in which beginners in a field of work are hired? Or is it an intermediate or advanced level? Sometimes this is indicated by such words as "Junior" or "Senior" in the class title. Other jurisdictions use Roman numerals to designate the level – Clerk I, Clerk II, for example. The word "Supervisor" sometimes appears in the title. If the level is not indicated by the title, check the description of duties. Will you be working under very close supervision, or will you have responsibility for independent decisions in this work?

4) Choose appropriate study materials

Now that you know the subjects to be examined and the relative amount of each subject to be covered, you can choose suitable study materials. For beginning level jobs, or even advanced ones, if you have a pronounced weakness in some aspect of your training, read a modern, standard textbook in that field. Be sure it is up to date and has general coverage. Such books are normally available at your library, and the librarian will be glad to help you locate one. For entry-level positions, questions of appropriate difficulty are chosen – neither highly advanced questions, nor those too simple. Such questions require careful thought but not advanced training.

If the position for which you are applying is technical or advanced, you will read more advanced, specialized material. If you are already familiar with the basic principles of your field, elementary textbooks would waste your time. Concentrate on advanced textbooks and technical periodicals. Think through the concepts and review difficult problems in your field.

These are all general sources. You can get more ideas on your own initiative, following these leads. For example, training manuals and publications of the government agency which employs workers in your field can be useful, particularly for technical and professional positions. A letter or visit to the government department involved may result in more specific study suggestions, and certainly will provide you with a more definite idea of the exact nature of the position you are seeking.

III. KINDS OF TESTS

Tests are used for purposes other than measuring knowledge and ability to perform specified duties. For some positions, it is equally important to test ability to make adjustments to new situations or to profit from training. In others, basic mental abilities not dependent on information are essential. Questions which test these things may not appear as pertinent to the duties of the position as those which test for knowledge and information. Yet they are often highly important parts of a fair examination. For very general questions, it is almost impossible to help you direct your study efforts. What we can do is to point out some of the more common of these general abilities needed in public service positions and describe some typical questions.

1) General information

Broad, general information has been found useful for predicting job success in some kinds of work. This is tested in a variety of ways, from vocabulary lists to questions about current events. Basic background in some field of work, such as sociology or economics, may be sampled in a group of questions. Often these are principles which have become familiar to most persons through exposure rather than through formal training. It is difficult to advise you how to study for these questions; being alert to the world around you is our best suggestion.

2) Verbal ability

An example of an ability needed in many positions is verbal or language ability. Verbal ability is, in brief, the ability to use and understand words. Vocabulary and grammar tests are typical measures of this ability. Reading comprehension or paragraph interpretation questions are common in many kinds of civil service tests. You are given a paragraph of written material and asked to find its central meaning.

3) Numerical ability

Number skills can be tested by the familiar arithmetic problem, by checking paired lists of numbers to see which are alike and which are different, or by interpreting charts and graphs. In the latter test, a graph may be printed in the test booklet which you are asked to use as the basis for answering questions.

4) Observation

A popular test for law-enforcement positions is the observation test. A picture is shown to you for several minutes, then taken away. Questions about the picture test your ability to observe both details and larger elements.

5) Following directions

In many positions in the public service, the employee must be able to carry out written instructions dependably and accurately. You may be given a chart with several columns, each column listing a variety of information. The questions require you to carry out directions involving the information given in the chart.

6) Skills and aptitudes

Performance tests effectively measure some manual skills and aptitudes. When the skill is one in which you are trained, such as typing or shorthand, you can practice. These tests are often very much like those given in business school or high school courses. For many of the other skills and aptitudes, however, no short-time preparation can be made. Skills and abilities natural to you or that you have developed throughout your lifetime are being tested.

Many of the general questions just described provide all the data needed to answer the questions and ask you to use your reasoning ability to find the answers. Your best preparation for these tests, as well as for tests of facts and ideas, is to be at your physical and mental best. You, no doubt, have your own methods of getting into an exam-taking mood and keeping "in shape." The next section lists some ideas on this subject.

IV. KINDS OF QUESTIONS

Only rarely is the "essay" question, which you answer in narrative form, used in civil service tests. Civil service tests are usually of the short-answer type. Full instructions for answering these questions will be given to you at the examination. But in case this is your first experience with short-answer questions and separate answer sheets, here is what you need to know:

1) Multiple-choice Questions

Most popular of the short-answer questions is the "multiple choice" or "best answer" question. It can be used, for example, to test for factual knowledge, ability to solve problems or judgment in meeting situations found at work.

A multiple-choice question is normally one of three types—

- It can begin with an incomplete statement followed by several possible endings. You are to find the one ending which *best* completes the statement, although some of the others may not be entirely wrong.
- It can also be a complete statement in the form of a question which is answered by choosing one of the statements listed.

- It can be in the form of a problem – again you select the best answer.

Here is an example of a multiple-choice question with a discussion which should give you some clues as to the method for choosing the right answer:

When an employee has a complaint about his assignment, the action which will *best* help him overcome his difficulty is to
    A. discuss his difficulty with his coworkers
    B. take the problem to the head of the organization
    C. take the problem to the person who gave him the assignment
    D. say nothing to anyone about his complaint

In answering this question, you should study each of the choices to find which is best. Consider choice "A" – Certainly an employee may discuss his complaint with fellow employees, but no change or improvement can result, and the complaint remains unresolved. Choice "B" is a poor choice since the head of the organization probably does not know what assignment you have been given, and taking your problem to him is known as "going over the head" of the supervisor. The supervisor, or person who made the assignment, is the person who can clarify it or correct any injustice. Choice "C" is, therefore, correct. To say nothing, as in choice "D," is unwise. Supervisors have and interest in knowing the problems employees are facing, and the employee is seeking a solution to his problem.

2) True/False Questions

The "true/false" or "right/wrong" form of question is sometimes used. Here a complete statement is given. Your job is to decide whether the statement is right or wrong.

SAMPLE: A roaming cell-phone call to a nearby city costs less than a non-roaming call to a distant city.

This statement is wrong, or false, since roaming calls are more expensive.

This is not a complete list of all possible question forms, although most of the others are variations of these common types. You will always get complete directions for answering questions. Be sure you understand *how* to mark your answers – ask questions until you do.

V. RECORDING YOUR ANSWERS

Computer terminals are used more and more today for many different kinds of exams.

For an examination with very few applicants, you may be told to record your answers in the test booklet itself. Separate answer sheets are much more common. If this separate answer sheet is to be scored by machine – and this is often the case – it is highly important that you mark your answers correctly in order to get credit.

An electronic scoring machine is often used in civil service offices because of the speed with which papers can be scored. Machine-scored answer sheets must be marked with a pencil, which will be given to you. This pencil has a high graphite content which responds to the electronic scoring machine. As a matter of fact, stray dots may register as answers, so do not let your pencil rest on the answer sheet while you are pondering the correct answer. Also, if your pencil lead breaks or is otherwise defective, ask for another.

Since the answer sheet will be dropped in a slot in the scoring machine, be careful not to bend the corners or get the paper crumpled.

The answer sheet normally has five vertical columns of numbers, with 30 numbers to a column. These numbers correspond to the question numbers in your test booklet. After each number, going across the page are four or five pairs of dotted lines. These short dotted lines have small letters or numbers above them. The first two pairs may also have a "T" or "F" above the letters. This indicates that the first two pairs only are to be used if the questions are of the true-false type. If the questions are multiple choice, disregard the "T" and "F" and pay attention only to the small letters or numbers.

Answer your questions in the manner of the sample that follows:

32. The largest city in the United States is
    A. Washington, D.C.
    B. New York City
    C. Chicago
    D. Detroit
    E. San Francisco

1) Choose the answer you think is best. (New York City is the largest, so "B" is correct.)
2) Find the row of dotted lines numbered the same as the question you are answering. (Find row number 32)
3) Find the pair of dotted lines corresponding to the answer. (Find the pair of lines under the mark "B.")
4) Make a solid black mark between the dotted lines.

VI. BEFORE THE TEST

Common sense will help you find procedures to follow to get ready for an examination. Too many of us, however, overlook these sensible measures. Indeed, nervousness and fatigue have been found to be the most serious reasons why applicants fail to do their best on civil service tests. Here is a list of reminders:

- Begin your preparation early – Don't wait until the last minute to go scurrying around for books and materials or to find out what the position is all about.
- Prepare continuously – An hour a night for a week is better than an all-night cram session. This has been definitely established. What is more, a night a week for a month will return better dividends than crowding your study into a shorter period of time.
- Locate the place of the exam – You have been sent a notice telling you when and where to report for the examination. If the location is in a different town or otherwise unfamiliar to you, it would be well to inquire the best route and learn something about the building.
- Relax the night before the test – Allow your mind to rest. Do not study at all that night. Plan some mild recreation or diversion; then go to bed early and get a good night's sleep.
- Get up early enough to make a leisurely trip to the place for the test – This way unforeseen events, traffic snarls, unfamiliar buildings, etc. will not upset you.
- Dress comfortably – A written test is not a fashion show. You will be known by number and not by name, so wear something comfortable.

- Leave excess paraphernalia at home – Shopping bags and odd bundles will get in your way. You need bring only the items mentioned in the official notice you received; usually everything you need is provided. Do not bring reference books to the exam. They will only confuse those last minutes and be taken away from you when in the test room.
- Arrive somewhat ahead of time – If because of transportation schedules you must get there very early, bring a newspaper or magazine to take your mind off yourself while waiting.
- Locate the examination room – When you have found the proper room, you will be directed to the seat or part of the room where you will sit. Sometimes you are given a sheet of instructions to read while you are waiting. Do not fill out any forms until you are told to do so; just read them and be prepared.
- Relax and prepare to listen to the instructions
- If you have any physical problem that may keep you from doing your best, be sure to tell the test administrator. If you are sick or in poor health, you really cannot do your best on the exam. You can come back and take the test some other time.

VII. AT THE TEST

The day of the test is here and you have the test booklet in your hand. The temptation to get going is very strong. Caution! There is more to success than knowing the right answers. You must know how to identify your papers and understand variations in the type of short-answer question used in this particular examination. Follow these suggestions for maximum results from your efforts:

1) Cooperate with the monitor
The test administrator has a duty to create a situation in which you can be as much at ease as possible. He will give instructions, tell you when to begin, check to see that you are marking your answer sheet correctly, and so on. He is not there to guard you, although he will see that your competitors do not take unfair advantage. He wants to help you do your best.

2) Listen to all instructions
Don't jump the gun! Wait until you understand all directions. In most civil service tests you get more time than you need to answer the questions. So don't be in a hurry. Read each word of instructions until you clearly understand the meaning. Study the examples, listen to all announcements and follow directions. Ask questions if you do not understand what to do.

3) Identify your papers
Civil service exams are usually identified by number only. You will be assigned a number; you must not put your name on your test papers. Be sure to copy your number correctly. Since more than one exam may be given, copy your exact examination title.

4) Plan your time
Unless you are told that a test is a "speed" or "rate of work" test, speed itself is usually not important. Time enough to answer all the questions will be provided, but this does not mean that you have all day. An overall time limit has been set. Divide the total time (in minutes) by the number of questions to determine the approximate time you have for each question.

5) Do not linger over difficult questions

If you come across a difficult question, mark it with a paper clip (useful to have along) and come back to it when you have been through the booklet. One caution if you do this – be sure to skip a number on your answer sheet as well. Check often to be sure that you have not lost your place and that you are marking in the row numbered the same as the question you are answering.

6) Read the questions

Be sure you know what the question asks! Many capable people are unsuccessful because they failed to *read* the questions correctly.

7) Answer all questions

Unless you have been instructed that a penalty will be deducted for incorrect answers, it is better to guess than to omit a question.

8) Speed tests

It is often better NOT to guess on speed tests. It has been found that on timed tests people are tempted to spend the last few seconds before time is called in marking answers at random – without even reading them – in the hope of picking up a few extra points. To discourage this practice, the instructions may warn you that your score will be "corrected" for guessing. That is, a penalty will be applied. The incorrect answers will be deducted from the correct ones, or some other penalty formula will be used.

9) Review your answers

If you finish before time is called, go back to the questions you guessed or omitted to give them further thought. Review other answers if you have time.

10) Return your test materials

If you are ready to leave before others have finished or time is called, take ALL your materials to the monitor and leave quietly. Never take any test material with you. The monitor can discover whose papers are not complete, and taking a test booklet may be grounds for disqualification.

VIII. EXAMINATION TECHNIQUES

1) Read the general instructions carefully. These are usually printed on the first page of the exam booklet. As a rule, these instructions refer to the timing of the examination; the fact that you should not start work until the signal and must stop work at a signal, etc. If there are any *special* instructions, such as a choice of questions to be answered, make sure that you note this instruction carefully.

2) When you are ready to start work on the examination, that is as soon as the signal has been given, read the instructions to each question booklet, underline any key words or phrases, such as *least, best, outline, describe* and the like. In this way you will tend to answer as requested rather than discover on reviewing your paper that you *listed without describing*, that you selected the *worst* choice rather than the *best* choice, etc.

3) If the examination is of the objective or multiple-choice type – that is, each question will also give a series of possible answers: A, B, C or D, and you are called upon to select the best answer and write the letter next to that answer on your answer paper – it is advisable to start answering each question in turn. There may be anywhere from 50 to 100 such questions in the three or four hours allotted and you can see how much time would be taken if you read through all the questions before beginning to answer any. Furthermore, if you come across a question or group of questions which you know would be difficult to answer, it would undoubtedly affect your handling of all the other questions.

4) If the examination is of the essay type and contains but a few questions, it is a moot point as to whether you should read all the questions before starting to answer any one. Of course, if you are given a choice – say five out of seven and the like – then it is essential to read all the questions so you can eliminate the two that are most difficult. If, however, you are asked to answer all the questions, there may be danger in trying to answer the easiest one first because you may find that you will spend too much time on it. The best technique is to answer the first question, then proceed to the second, etc.

5) Time your answers. Before the exam begins, write down the time it started, then add the time allowed for the examination and write down the time it must be completed, then divide the time available somewhat as follows:
   - If 3-1/2 hours are allowed, that would be 210 minutes. If you have 80 objective-type questions, that would be an average of 2-1/2 minutes per question. Allow yourself no more than 2 minutes per question, or a total of 160 minutes, which will permit about 50 minutes to review.
   - If for the time allotment of 210 minutes there are 7 essay questions to answer, that would average about 30 minutes a question. Give yourself only 25 minutes per question so that you have about 35 minutes to review.

6) The most important instruction is to *read each question* and make sure you know what is wanted. The second most important instruction is to *time yourself properly* so that you answer every question. The third most important instruction is to *answer every question*. Guess if you have to but include something for each question. Remember that you will receive no credit for a blank and will probably receive some credit if you write something in answer to an essay question. If you guess a letter – say "B" for a multiple-choice question – you may have guessed right. If you leave a blank as an answer to a multiple-choice question, the examiners may respect your feelings but it will not add a point to your score. Some exams may penalize you for wrong answers, so in such cases *only*, you may not want to guess unless you have some basis for your answer.

7) Suggestions
   a. Objective-type questions
      1. Examine the question booklet for proper sequence of pages and questions
      2. Read all instructions carefully
      3. Skip any question which seems too difficult; return to it after all other questions have been answered
      4. Apportion your time properly; do not spend too much time on any single question or group of questions

5. Note and underline key words – *all, most, fewest, least, best, worst, same, opposite,* etc.
6. Pay particular attention to negatives
7. Note unusual option, e.g., unduly long, short, complex, different or similar in content to the body of the question
8. Observe the use of "hedging" words – *probably, may, most likely,* etc.
9. Make sure that your answer is put next to the same number as the question
10. Do not second-guess unless you have good reason to believe the second answer is definitely more correct
11. Cross out original answer if you decide another answer is more accurate; do not erase until you are ready to hand your paper in
12. Answer all questions; guess unless instructed otherwise
13. Leave time for review

    b. Essay questions
1. Read each question carefully
2. Determine exactly what is wanted. Underline key words or phrases.
3. Decide on outline or paragraph answer
4. Include many different points and elements unless asked to develop any one or two points or elements
5. Show impartiality by giving pros and cons unless directed to select one side only
6. Make and write down any assumptions you find necessary to answer the questions
7. Watch your English, grammar, punctuation and choice of words
8. Time your answers; don't crowd material

8) Answering the essay question

Most essay questions can be answered by framing the specific response around several key words or ideas. Here are a few such key words or ideas:

M's: manpower, materials, methods, money, management
P's: purpose, program, policy, plan, procedure, practice, problems, pitfalls, personnel, public relations
    a. Six basic steps in handling problems:
1. Preliminary plan and background development
2. Collect information, data and facts
3. Analyze and interpret information, data and facts
4. Analyze and develop solutions as well as make recommendations
5. Prepare report and sell recommendations
6. Install recommendations and follow up effectiveness

    b. Pitfalls to avoid
1. *Taking things for granted* – A statement of the situation does not necessarily imply that each of the elements is necessarily true; for example, a complaint may be invalid and biased so that all that can be taken for granted is that a complaint has been registered

2. *Considering only one side of a situation* – Wherever possible, indicate several alternatives and then point out the reasons you selected the best one
3. *Failing to indicate follow up* – Whenever your answer indicates action on your part, make certain that you will take proper follow-up action to see how successful your recommendations, procedures or actions turn out to be
4. *Taking too long in answering any single question* – Remember to time your answers properly

IX. AFTER THE TEST

Scoring procedures differ in detail among civil service jurisdictions although the general principles are the same. Whether the papers are hand-scored or graded by machine we have described, they are nearly always graded by number. That is, the person who marks the paper knows only the number – never the name – of the applicant. Not until all the papers have been graded will they be matched with names. If other tests, such as training and experience or oral interview ratings have been given, scores will be combined. Different parts of the examination usually have different weights. For example, the written test might count 60 percent of the final grade, and a rating of training and experience 40 percent. In many jurisdictions, veterans will have a certain number of points added to their grades.

After the final grade has been determined, the names are placed in grade order and an eligible list is established. There are various methods for resolving ties between those who get the same final grade – probably the most common is to place first the name of the person whose application was received first. Job offers are made from the eligible list in the order the names appear on it. You will be notified of your grade and your rank as soon as all these computations have been made. This will be done as rapidly as possible.

People who are found to meet the requirements in the announcement are called "eligibles." Their names are put on a list of eligible candidates. An eligible's chances of getting a job depend on how high he stands on this list and how fast agencies are filling jobs from the list.

When a job is to be filled from a list of eligibles, the agency asks for the names of people on the list of eligibles for that job. When the civil service commission receives this request, it sends to the agency the names of the three people highest on this list. Or, if the job to be filled has specialized requirements, the office sends the agency the names of the top three persons who meet these requirements from the general list.

The appointing officer makes a choice from among the three people whose names were sent to him. If the selected person accepts the appointment, the names of the others are put back on the list to be considered for future openings.

That is the rule in hiring from all kinds of eligible lists, whether they are for typist, carpenter, chemist, or something else. For every vacancy, the appointing officer has his choice of any one of the top three eligibles on the list. This explains why the person whose name is on top of the list sometimes does not get an appointment when some of the persons lower on the list do. If the appointing officer chooses the second or third eligible, the No. 1 eligible does not get a job at once, but stays on the list until he is appointed or the list is terminated.

X. HOW TO PASS THE INTERVIEW TEST

The examination for which you applied requires an oral interview test. You have already taken the written test and you are now being called for the interview test – the final part of the formal examination.

You may think that it is not possible to prepare for an interview test and that there are no procedures to follow during an interview. Our purpose is to point out some things you can do in advance that will help you and some good rules to follow and pitfalls to avoid while you are being interviewed.

What is an interview supposed to test?

The written examination is designed to test the technical knowledge and competence of the candidate; the oral is designed to evaluate intangible qualities, not readily measured otherwise, and to establish a list showing the relative fitness of each candidate – as measured against his competitors – for the position sought. Scoring is not on the basis of "right" and "wrong," but on a sliding scale of values ranging from "not passable" to "outstanding." As a matter of fact, it is possible to achieve a relatively low score without a single "incorrect" answer because of evident weakness in the qualities being measured.

Occasionally, an examination may consist entirely of an oral test – either an individual or a group oral. In such cases, information is sought concerning the technical knowledges and abilities of the candidate, since there has been no written examination for this purpose. More commonly, however, an oral test is used to supplement a written examination.

Who conducts interviews?

The composition of oral boards varies among different jurisdictions. In nearly all, a representative of the personnel department serves as chairman. One of the members of the board may be a representative of the department in which the candidate would work. In some cases, "outside experts" are used, and, frequently, a businessman or some other representative of the general public is asked to serve. Labor and management or other special groups may be represented. The aim is to secure the services of experts in the appropriate field.

However the board is composed, it is a good idea (and not at all improper or unethical) to ascertain in advance of the interview who the members are and what groups they represent. When you are introduced to them, you will have some idea of their backgrounds and interests, and at least you will not stutter and stammer over their names.

What should be done before the interview?

While knowledge about the board members is useful and takes some of the surprise element out of the interview, there is other preparation which is more substantive. It *is* possible to prepare for an oral interview – in several ways:

1) Keep a copy of your application and review it carefully before the interview

This may be the only document before the oral board, and the starting point of the interview. Know what education and experience you have listed there, and the sequence and dates of all of it. Sometimes the board will ask you to review the highlights of your experience for them; you should not have to hem and haw doing it.

2) Study the class specification and the examination announcement

Usually, the oral board has one or both of these to guide them. The qualities, characteristics or knowledges required by the position sought are stated in these documents. They offer valuable clues as to the nature of the oral interview. For example, if the job involves supervisory responsibilities, the announcement will usually indicate that knowledge of modern supervisory methods and the qualifications of the candidate as a supervisor will be tested. If so, you can expect such questions, frequently in the form of a hypothetical situation which you are expected to solve. NEVER go into an oral without knowledge of the duties and responsibilities of the job you seek.

3) Think through each qualification required

Try to visualize the kind of questions you would ask if you were a board member. How well could you answer them? Try especially to appraise your own knowledge and background in each area, *measured against the job sought*, and identify any areas in which you are weak. Be critical and realistic – do not flatter yourself.

4) Do some general reading in areas in which you feel you may be weak

For example, if the job involves supervision and your past experience has NOT, some general reading in supervisory methods and practices, particularly in the field of human relations, might be useful. Do NOT study agency procedures or detailed manuals. The oral board will be testing your understanding and capacity, not your memory.

5) Get a good night's sleep and watch your general health and mental attitude

You will want a clear head at the interview. Take care of a cold or any other minor ailment, and of course, no hangovers.

What should be done on the day of the interview?

Now comes the day of the interview itself. Give yourself plenty of time to get there. Plan to arrive somewhat ahead of the scheduled time, particularly if your appointment is in the fore part of the day. If a previous candidate fails to appear, the board might be ready for you a bit early. By early afternoon an oral board is almost invariably behind schedule if there are many candidates, and you may have to wait. Take along a book or magazine to read, or your application to review, but leave any extraneous material in the waiting room when you go in for your interview. In any event, relax and compose yourself.

The matter of dress is important. The board is forming impressions about you – from your experience, your manners, your attitude, and your appearance. Give your personal appearance careful attention. Dress your best, but not your flashiest. Choose conservative, appropriate clothing, and be sure it is immaculate. This is a business interview, and your appearance should indicate that you regard it as such. Besides, being well groomed and properly dressed will help boost your confidence.

Sooner or later, someone will call your name and escort you into the interview room. *This is it.* From here on you are on your own. It is too late for any more preparation. But remember, you asked for this opportunity to prove your fitness, and you are here because your request was granted.

What happens when you go in?

The usual sequence of events will be as follows: The clerk (who is often the board stenographer) will introduce you to the chairman of the oral board, who will introduce you to the other members of the board. Acknowledge the introductions before you sit down. Do not be surprised if you find a microphone facing you or a stenotypist sitting by. Oral interviews are usually recorded in the event of an appeal or other review.

Usually the chairman of the board will open the interview by reviewing the highlights of your education and work experience from your application – primarily for the benefit of the other members of the board, as well as to get the material into the record. Do not interrupt or comment unless there is an error or significant misinterpretation; if that is the case, do not hesitate. But do not quibble about insignificant matters. Also, he will usually ask you some question about your education, experience or your present job – partly to get you to start talking and to establish the interviewing "rapport." He may start the actual questioning, or turn it over to one of the other members. Frequently, each member undertakes the questioning on a particular area, one in which he is perhaps most competent, so you can expect each member to participate in the examination. Because time is limited, you may also expect some rather abrupt switches in the direction the questioning takes, so do not be upset by it. Normally, a board member will not pursue a single line of questioning unless he discovers a particular strength or weakness.

After each member has participated, the chairman will usually ask whether any member has any further questions, then will ask you if you have anything you wish to add. Unless you are expecting this question, it may floor you. Worse, it may start you off on an extended, extemporaneous speech. The board is not usually seeking more information. The question is principally to offer you a last opportunity to present further qualifications or to indicate that you have nothing to add. So, if you feel that a significant qualification or characteristic has been overlooked, it is proper to point it out in a sentence or so. Do not compliment the board on the thoroughness of their examination – they have been sketchy, and you know it. If you wish, merely say, "No thank you, I have nothing further to add." This is a point where you can "talk yourself out" of a good impression or fail to present an important bit of information. Remember, *you close the interview yourself.*

The chairman will then say, "That is all, Mr. _____, thank you." Do not be startled; the interview is over, and quicker than you think. Thank him, gather your belongings and take your leave. Save your sigh of relief for the other side of the door.

How to put your best foot forward
Throughout this entire process, you may feel that the board individually and collectively is trying to pierce your defenses, seek out your hidden weaknesses and embarrass and confuse you. Actually, this is not true. They are obliged to make an appraisal of your qualifications for the job you are seeking, and they want to see you in your best light. Remember, they must interview all candidates and a non-cooperative candidate may become a failure in spite of their best efforts to bring out his qualifications. Here are 15 suggestions that will help you:

1) Be natural – Keep your attitude confident, not cocky
If you are not confident that you can do the job, do not expect the board to be. Do not apologize for your weaknesses, try to bring out your strong points. The board is interested in a positive, not negative, presentation. Cockiness will antagonize any board member and make him wonder if you are covering up a weakness by a false show of strength.

2) Get comfortable, but don't lounge or sprawl
Sit erectly but not stiffly. A careless posture may lead the board to conclude that you are careless in other things, or at least that you are not impressed by the importance of the occasion. Either conclusion is natural, even if incorrect. Do not fuss with your clothing, a pencil or an ashtray. Your hands may occasionally be useful to emphasize a point; do not let them become a point of distraction.

3) Do not wisecrack or make small talk
This is a serious situation, and your attitude should show that you consider it as such. Further, the time of the board is limited – they do not want to waste it, and neither should you.

4) Do not exaggerate your experience or abilities

In the first place, from information in the application or other interviews and sources, the board may know more about you than you think. Secondly, you probably will not get away with it. An experienced board is rather adept at spotting such a situation, so do not take the chance.

5) If you know a board member, do not make a point of it, yet do not hide it

Certainly you are not fooling him, and probably not the other members of the board. Do not try to take advantage of your acquaintanceship – it will probably do you little good.

6) Do not dominate the interview

Let the board do that. They will give you the clues – do not assume that you have to do all the talking. Realize that the board has a number of questions to ask you, and do not try to take up all the interview time by showing off your extensive knowledge of the answer to the first one.

7) Be attentive

You only have 20 minutes or so, and you should keep your attention at its sharpest throughout. When a member is addressing a problem or question to you, give him your undivided attention. Address your reply principally to him, but do not exclude the other board members.

8) Do not interrupt

A board member may be stating a problem for you to analyze. He will ask you a question when the time comes. Let him state the problem, and wait for the question.

9) Make sure you understand the question

Do not try to answer until you are sure what the question is. If it is not clear, restate it in your own words or ask the board member to clarify it for you. However, do not haggle about minor elements.

10) Reply promptly but not hastily

A common entry on oral board rating sheets is "candidate responded readily," or "candidate hesitated in replies." Respond as promptly and quickly as you can, but do not jump to a hasty, ill-considered answer.

11) Do not be peremptory in your answers

A brief answer is proper – but do not fire your answer back. That is a losing game from your point of view. The board member can probably ask questions much faster than you can answer them.

12) Do not try to create the answer you think the board member wants

He is interested in what kind of mind you have and how it works – not in playing games. Furthermore, he can usually spot this practice and will actually grade you down on it.

13) Do not switch sides in your reply merely to agree with a board member

Frequently, a member will take a contrary position merely to draw you out and to see if you are willing and able to defend your point of view. Do not start a debate, yet do not surrender a good position. If a position is worth taking, it is worth defending.

14) Do not be afraid to admit an error in judgment if you are shown to be wrong

   The board knows that you are forced to reply without any opportunity for careful consideration. Your answer may be demonstrably wrong. If so, admit it and get on with the interview.

15) Do not dwell at length on your present job

   The opening question may relate to your present assignment. Answer the question but do not go into an extended discussion. You are being examined for a *new* job, not your present one. As a matter of fact, try to phrase ALL your answers in terms of the job for which you are being examined.

Basis of Rating

   Probably you will forget most of these "do's" and "don'ts" when you walk into the oral interview room. Even remembering them all will not ensure you a passing grade. Perhaps you did not have the qualifications in the first place. But remembering them will help you to put your best foot forward, without treading on the toes of the board members.

   Rumor and popular opinion to the contrary notwithstanding, an oral board wants you to make the best appearance possible. They know you are under pressure – but they also want to see how you respond to it as a guide to what your reaction would be under the pressures of the job you seek. They will be influenced by the degree of poise you display, the personal traits you show and the manner in which you respond.

ABOUT THIS BOOK

   This book contains tests divided into Examination Sections. Go through each test, answering every question in the margin. We have also attached a sample answer sheet at the back of the book that can be removed and used. At the end of each test look at the answer key and check your answers. On the ones you got wrong, look at the right answer choice and learn. Do not fill in the answers first. Do not memorize the questions and answers, but understand the answer and principles involved. On your test, the questions will likely be different from the samples. Questions are changed and new ones added. If you understand these past questions you should have success with any changes that arise. Tests may consist of several types of questions. We have additional books on each subject should more study be advisable or necessary for you. Finally, the more you study, the better prepared you will be. This book is intended to be the last thing you study before you walk into the examination room. Prior study of relevant texts is also recommended. NLC publishes some of these in our Fundamental Series. Knowledge and good sense are important factors in passing your exam. Good luck also helps. So now study this Passbook, absorb the material contained within and take that knowledge into the examination. Then do your best to pass that exam.

———

EXAMINATION SECTION

EXAMINATION SECTION
TEST 1

DIRECTIONS: Each question or incomplete statement is followed by several suggested answers or completions. Select the one that BEST answers the question or completes the statement. *PRINT THE LETTER OF THE CORRECT ANSWER IN THE SPACE AT THE RIGHT.*

1. A law enforcement officer may make an arrest without a warrant when the crime   1.____

    A. is committed in his presence
    B. violates airport security
    C. takes place in a sterile area
    D. takes place in an exclusive area
    E. all of the above

2. A private security force must have _____ in order to perform the law enforcement func-   2.____
tion.

    A. arrest power
    B. a warrant
    C. written agreement between the employer and the airport operator
    D. local approval
    E. firearms

3. Alternate security procedures to be used during emergencies are to be included in the   3.____
security program when

    A. ordinary procedures are insufficient
    B. the airport operator has developed alternate procedures
    C. alternate procedures include the use of locally deputized law enforcement officers
    D. the FAA requires the airport operator to go to unreasonable extremes to meet all
        possible security threats
    E. at all times

4. Disclosure of the airport security program may be prohibited if it   4.____

    A. contains sensitive information
    B. will be of value to those who would commit offenses against civil aviation
    C. would be detrimental to the safety of persons traveling in air transportation
    D. involves national security
    E. is not in conflict with the Freedom of Information Act

5. The portion of an airport designed and used for landing, take-offs, or surface maneuver-   5.____
ing of airplanes, is called the _____ area.

    A. general aviation   B. air operations   C. exclusive
    D. sterile   E. ground

6. Airport security programs provide for the safety of persons and property against   6.____

    A. threats of violence
    B. violations of civil liberties
    C. any and all damages connected with air transportation

D. acts of criminal violence and aircraft piracy
E. hijacking

7. The air carrier should notify the _____ when the procedures, facilities and equipment it uses over an exclusive area are inadequate.   7._____

    A. Regional Director
    B. Law Enforcement Officer
    C. Airport Operator
    D. Civil Aviation Security Inspector
    E. Administrator

8. Each airport operator shall maintain at LEAST one complete copy of its approved security program at   8._____

    A. the Department of Justice
    B. the entrance to each sterile area
    C. the officer of any Civil Aviation Security Inspector
    D. the office of the Regional Director
    E. its principal operations office

9. _____ days are allowed for the approval of a security program?   9._____

    A. 15   B. 30   C. 45   D. 60   E. 90

10. Proposed amendments to the security program must   10._____

    A. be distributed to the air carrier tenants
    B. receive the oral approval of the air carrier tenants
    C. receive written approval of the air carrier tenants
    D. be coordinated with the air carrier tenants
    E. not have any involvement with the air carrier tenants

11. The Airport Operator must _____ access to each air operations area.   11._____

    A. prevent   B. allow   C. forbid
    D. control   E. guard

12. The _____ MOST directly depends on the volume of passenger traffic and the configuration of the terminal screening point.   12._____

    A. response time of the law enforcement officers
    B. number of law enforcement officers
    C. type of security devices required
    D. nature of the law enforcement response
    E. specific form of law enforcement presence

13. One person carrying out both the screening process and the law enforcement function may be an adequate security measure   13._____

    A. when cost is a factor
    B. at certain small airports
    C. at low risk airports
    D. for planes of a certain seating configuration
    E. in no case

14. The training program of law enforcement officers should be based on   14._____

    A. state or local training standards
    B. minimum requirements of basic military training
    C. the broadest spectrum of police duties
    D. uniform FAA standards
    E. the specific needs of the individual airport

15. A weapon found at the airport other than in the screening point, or within a sterile area, is   15._____
subject to

    A. FAA authority   B. highway patrol
    C. local law   D. flight security
    E. federal law

16. A change in _____ would NOT necessitate amending the security program.   16._____

    A. facilities or equipment
    B. an alternate security procedure
    C. law enforcement support
    D. system for maintaining records
    E. none of the above

17. After notification of the proper office of a changed condition affecting security, an amend-   17._____
ment must be submitted for approval

    A. at the same time as notification
    B. within 10 days
    C. within 15 days
    D. within 30 days
    E. within 60 days

18. A proposed security amendment may be approved or   18._____

    A. denied
    B. modified, or denied
    C. modified, or transferred
    D. denied, or transferred
    E. denied, or a "pocket" denial issued

19. The FIRST step in the disposition of a petition for reconsideration of a denied amend-   19._____
ment of a security program is

    A. approval or affirming denial
    B. approval or transfer
    C. modification or affirming denial
    D. affirming denial or transfer
    E. affirming denial or "pocket" denial

20. The FAA notifies the _____ of an amendment it has adopted.   20._____

    A. Regional Director   B. Municipal government
    C. Airport Operator   D. air carriers
    E. Administrator

21. Upon receipt of a petition for reconsideration of an amendment adopted by the FAA, the Regional Director may 21.____

    A. rescind or modify the amendment
    B. rescind, modify, or issue the amendment as proposed
    C. rescind, issue as proposed, or transfer the petition
    D. issue as proposed, or transfer the petition
    E. rescind, modify, or transfer the petition

22. An amendment of a security program by the FAA requiring emergency action ALWAYS contains 22.____

    A. a stated period of effectiveness
    B. alternate security procedures
    C. a statement of the reasons for the emergency
    D. the power to deputize persons to arrest for both local and federal offenses
    E. all of the above

23. Each penetration of an air operations area by an unauthorized person must NOT be 23.____

    A. prevented
    B. proved and witnessed
    C. proved and repelled
    D. promptly detected and controlled
    E. prohibited

24. Which law enforcement officers are exempt from completing a training program? 24.____

    A. Local or state policemen
    B. Private law enforcement personnel
    C. Locally deputized law enforcement officers
    D. Persons recently separated from military service
    E. None of the above

25. The role of airport security is to _____ criminal violence. 25.____

    A. prevent   B. control   C. circumvent
    D. detect   E. anticipate

26. A law enforcement officer must have authority to 26.____

    A. arrest on or off duty at the airport
    B. arrest while on duty at the airport
    C. arrest at or off the airport, on or off, duty
    D. arrest while on duty at the airport with a warrant
    E. arrest while, on or off duty at the airport, with or without, a warrant

27. In addition to meeting standards prescribed by either state or local jurisdiction, the training program for law enforcement officers includes training in 27.____

    A. use of firearms
    B. disarming bombs
    C. use of explosives and incendiary devices
    D. bomb detection
    E. undercover support

28. The FAA requires officers' attitudes toward persons subject to aviation security activities to be
    28.____

    A. authoritative   B. respectful   C. threatening
    D. courteous   E. understanding

29. The Airport Operator may request the use of additional law enforcement officers when
    29.____

    A. they are not available in sufficient numbers
    B. air carrier security over an exclusive area endangers the air operations area
    C. an emergency situation exists
    D. a threat has been received
    E. all of the above

30. Before requesting federal law enforcement officers, the Airport Operator must show
    30.____

    A. efforts to recruit additional personnel
    B. efforts to obtain law enforcement from state, local and private agencies
    C. a condition exists preventing use of state, local and private agencies
    D. the inadequacy of state, local and private agencies
    E. that a strike or job action situation exists

31. The cost of federal law enforcement officers used for airport security is the responsibility of the
    31.____

    A. FAA
    B. federal agency supplying them
    C. municipal district in which airport is located
    D. air carrier requesting use
    E. Airport Operator

32. Use of law enforcement officers for airport security that are employed by a federal agency other than the FAA requires the consent of the
    32.____

    A. Administrator   B. Regional Director
    C. Airport Operator   D. head of that agency
    E. Department of Transportation

33. Federal law enforcement officers used for airport security may be in the employ of
    33.____

    A. the FAA
    B. the Treasury Department
    C. the Transportation Department
    D. the Commerce Department
    E. any Federal agency

34. The MINIMUM period of time a record must be maintained is
    34.____

    A. 30 days   B. 60 days   C. 90 days   D. 1 year   E. 2 years

35. The airport operator need NOT include in his record
    35.____

    A. an actual bombing
    B. the number of real bombs found
    C. simulated bombs found

D. number of threats received
E. none of the above

36. FAA security regulations were originally designed to meet threats   36.____

    A. affecting national security
    B. of terrorist groups
    C. of hijacking
    D. involving carriage of firearms, explosives or incendiary devices
    E. of criminal violence

37. FAA security regulations were originally intended to protect   37.____

    A. commuter air carriers   B. foreign air carriers
    C. larger air terminals   D. route carriers
    E. wholly intrastate air carriers

38. A security program is required of an airplane with a seating configuration of 9 when the   38.____

    A. flight is intrastate
    B. flight is interstate
    C. FAA identifies a security threat
    D. passengers have controlled access to a sterile area
    E. passengers have uncontrolled access to a sterile area

39. The cost of security requirements may be higher for particular flights because of   39.____

    A. scheduling   B. airplane complexity
    C. capacity enplanements   D. vulnerable destinations
    E. limited enplanements

40. The increased security threat to the commuter industry since implementation of the   40.____
Deregulation Act is a result of the use of

    A. larger aircraft
    B. scheduled operations
    C. popular routes
    D. public charter operations
    E. there has been no increase

41. Potential hijackers would *most likely* consider   41.____

    A. route and range
    B. range and number of passengers
    C. schedule and destination
    D. route and destination
    E. carrier and destination

42. A general rule applicable to security requirements is that security is commensurate with   42.____

    A. the size of the airport
    B. the number of operations
    C. size of the air operations area
    D. the existing threat
    E. cost

43. A security screening system is required by an operator using airplanes with a seating capacity of 40 when 43.____

    A. passengers have uncontrolled access to an exclusive area
    B. passengers have controlled access to a sterile area
    C. no antihijacking crew training is available
    D. the FAA identifies a security threat
    E. at all times

44. Operators of airplanes may discharge unscreened passengers into a sterile area when 44.____

    A. their access is controlled through surveillance and escort procedures
    B. prior arrangement has been made with the FAA
    C. operators are not required to screen their passengers
    D. procedures are used to prevent or deter the introduction of explosives and incendiaries into the area
    E. at no time

45. Deplaning passengers are screened before entry into a sterile area when 45.____

    A. the airplane is unprotected
    B. the airplane operator was not previously required to screen them
    C. law enforcement support is not required
    D. the baggage claims area is located in a sterile area
    E. the airport operator requires it

46. Responsibility for establishing and implementing law enforcement arrangements at airports regularly serving smaller airplanes at which screening is not required is borne by the 46.____

    A. law enforcement agency   B. Airport Operator
    C. Regional Director   D. airplane operator
    E. airport security

47. Most of the costs of meeting contingency procedures due to a threat condition are associated with the cost of 47.____

    A. alterations to airport terminals
    B. metal detectors
    C. personnel
    D. x-ray machines
    E. training programs

48. The MOST frequent cause of a new security cost for the operator of smaller airplanes is 48.____

    A. meeting threat situations
    B. the desire to discharge passengers directly into a sterile area
    C. the desire to operate out of larger airports
    D. meeting FAA requirements
    E. the desire to become an FAA certificate holder

49. Interim measures instituted to maintain security under changed conditions remain in effect until   49.____

   A. an amendment to the security program is approved
   B. the FAA security office evaluates the situation
   C. the interim measures are approved
   D. the airport operator conducts his investigation
   E. the FAA security office proposes alternate measures

50. The FAA is authorized to prescribe regulations affecting activity   50.____

   A. in sterile areas
   B. in any area not designated "exclusive"
   C. aboard aircraft
   D. at the airport and aboard aircraft
   E. on areas adjacent to the airport, at the airport, and aboard aircraft

———

KEY (CORRECT ANSWERS)

1. A	11. D	21. E	31. E	41. B
2. A	12. E	22. C	32. D	42. D
3. B	13. B	23. B	33. E	43. D
4. C	14. A	24. E	34. C	44. A
5. B	15. C	25. B	35. E	45. B
6. D	16. D	26. B	36. C	46. D
7. C	17. D	27. A	37. D	47. C
8. E	18. A	28. D	38. E	48. B
9. B	19. B	29. A	39. E	49. A
10. E	20. C	30. B	40. E	50. D

———

EXAMINATION SECTION
TEST 1

DIRECTIONS: Each question or incomplete statement is followed by several suggested answers or completions. Select the one that BEST answers the question or completes the statement. *PRINT THE LETTER OF THE CORRECT ANSWER IN THE SPACE AT THE RIGHT.*

Questions 1-4.

DIRECTIONS: Questions 1 through 4 are based on the picture entitled *Contents of a Woman's Handbag.* Assume that all of the contents are shown in the picture.

CONTENTS OF A WOMAN'S HANDBAG

1. Where does Gladys Constantine live?   1.____

   A. Chalmers Street in Manhattan
   B. Summer Street in Manhattan
   C. Summer Street in Brooklyn
   D. Chalmers Street in Brooklyn

2. How many keys were in the handbag?   2.____

   A. 2   B. 3   C. 4   D. 5

3. How much money was in the handbag? _____ dollar(s).   3.____

   A. Exactly five   B. More than five
   C. Exactly ten   D. Less than one

4. The sales slip found in the handbag shows the purchase of which of the following?   4.____

   A. The handbag   B. Lipstick
   C. Tissues   D. Prescription medicine

Questions 5-8.

DIRECTIONS: Questions 5 through 8 are based on the floor plan below.

FLOOR PLAN

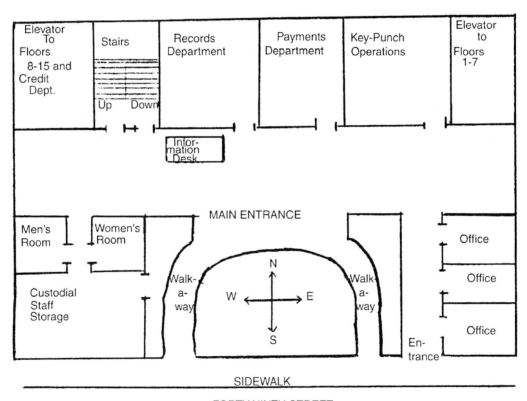

5. A special officer (security officer) on duty at the main entrance must be aware of other outside entrances to his area of the building. These unguarded entrances are usually kept locked, but they are important in case of fire or other emergency.
Besides the main entrance, how many OTHER entrances shown on the floor plan directly face Forty-ninth Street?
_____ other entrances.

   A. No   B. One   C. Two   D. Three

5._____

6. A person who arrives at the main entrance and asks to be directed to the Credit Department SHOULD be told to

   A. take the elevator on the left
   B. take the elevator on the right
   C. go to a different entrance
   D. go up the stairs on the left

6._____

7. On the east side of the entrance can be found

   A. a storage room   B. offices
   C. toilets   D. stairs

7._____

8. The space DIRECTLY BEHIND the Information Desk in the floor plan is occupied by

   A. up and down stairs   B. key punch operations
   C. toilets   D. the records department

8._____

Questions 9-12.

DIRECTIONS: Answer Questions 9 to 12 on the basis of the information given in the passage below.

The public often believes that the main job of a uniformed officer is to enforce laws by simply arresting people. In reality, however, many of the situations that an officer deals with do not call for the use of his arrest power. In the first place, an officer spends much of his time <u>preventing</u> crimes from happening, by spotting potential violations or suspicious behavior and taking action to prevent illegal acts. In the second place, many of the situations in which officers are called on for assistance involve elements like personal arguments, husband-wife quarrels, noisy juveniles, or mentally disturbed persons. The majority of these problems do not result in arrests and convictions, and often they do not even involve illegal behavior. In the third place, even in situations where there seems to be good reason to make an arrest, an officer may have to exercise very good judgment. There are times when making an arrest too soon could touch off a riot, or could result in the detention of a minor offender while major offenders escaped, or could cut short the gathering of necessary on-the-scene evidence.

9. The above passage IMPLIES that most citizens

   A. will start to riot if they see an arrest being made
   B. appreciate the work that law enforcement officers do
   C. do not realize that making arrests is only a small part of law enforcement
   D. never call for assistance unless they are involved in a personal argument or a husband-wife quarrel

9._____

10. According to the passage, one way in which law enforcement officers can prevent crimes   10.____
from happening is by

    A. arresting suspicious characters
    B. letting minor offenders go free
    C. taking action on potential violations
    D. refusing to get involved in husband-wife fights

11. According to the passage, which of the following statements is NOT true of situations   11.____
involving mentally disturbed persons?

    A. It is a waste of time to call on law enforcement officers for assistance in such situations.
    B. Such situations may not involve illegal behavior
    C. Such situations often do not result in arrests.
    D. Citizens often turn to law enforcement officers for help in such situations.

12. The last sentence in the passage mentions *detention of minor offenders.*   12.____
Of the following, which BEST explains the meaning of the word *detention* as used
here?

    A. Sentencing someone
    B. Indicting someone
    C. Calling someone before a grand jury
    D. Arresting someone

Questions 13-28.

DIRECTIONS: In answering Questions 13 through 28, assume that *you* means a special officer (security officer) on duty. Your basic responsibilities are safeguarding people and property and maintaining order in the area to which you are assigned. You are in uniform, and you are not armed. You keep in touch with your supervisory station either by telephone or by a two-way radio (walkie-talkie).

13. It is a general rule that if the security alarm goes off showing that someone has made an   13.____
unlawful entrance into a building, no officer responsible for security shall proceed to
investigate alone. Each officer must be accompanied by at least one other officer.
Of the following, which is the MOST probable reason for this rule?

    A. It is dangerous for an officer to investigate such a situation alone.
    B. The intruder might try to bribe an officer to let him go.
    C. One officer may be inexperienced and needs an experienced partner.
    D. Two officers are better than one officer in writing a report of the investigation.

14. You are on weekend duty on the main floor of a public building. The building is closed to   14.____
the public on weekends, but some employees are sometimes asked to work weekends.
You have been instructed to use cautious good judgment in opening the door for such
persons.
Of the following, which one MOST clearly shows the poorest judgment?

    A.   Admitting an employee who is personally known to you without asking to see any identification except the permit slip signed by the employee's supervisor

    B.   Refusing to admit someone whom you do not recognize but who claims left his identification at home

    C.   Admitting to the building only those who can give a detailed description of their weekend work duties

    D.   Leaving the entrance door locked for a while to make regulation security checks of other areas in the building with the result that no one can either enter or leave during these periods

15. You are on duty at a public building. An office employee tells you that she left her purse in her desk when she went out to lunch, and she has just discovered that it is gone. She has been back from lunch for half an hour and has not left her desk during this period. What should you do FIRST?   15._____

    A.   Warn all security personnel to stop any suspicious-looking person who is seen with a purse

    B.   Ask for a description of the purse

    C.   Call the Lost and Found and ask if a purse has been turned in

    D.   Obtain statements from any employees who were in the office during the lunch hour

16. You are patrolling your assigned area in a public building. You hear a sudden crash and the sound of running footsteps. You investigate and find that someone has forced open a locked entrance to the building. What is the FIRST thing you should do?   16._____

    A.   Close the door and try to fix the lock so that no one else can get in

    B.   Use your two-way radio to report the emergency and summon help

    C.   Chase after the person whose running footsteps you heard

    D.   Go immediately to your base office and make out a brief written report

17. You and another special officer (security officer) are on duty in the main waiting area at a welfare center. A caseworker calls both of you over and whispers that one of the clients, Richard Roe, may be carrying a gun. Of the following, what is the BEST action for both of you to take?   17._____

    A.   You should approach the man, one on each side, and one of you should say loudly and clearly, *"Richard Roe, you are under arrest."*

    B.   Both of you should ask the man to go with you to a private room, and then find out if he is carrying a gun

    C.   Both of you should grab him, handcuff him, and take him to the nearest precinct station house

    D.   Both of you should watch him carefully but not do anything unless he actually pulls a gun

18. You are on duty at a welfare center. You are told that a caseworker is being threatened by a man with a knife. You go immediately to the scene, and you find the caseworker lying on the floor with blood spurting from a wound in his arm. You do not know who the attacker is. What should you do FIRST?   18._____

    A.   Ask the caseworker for a description of the attacker so that you can set out in pursuit and try to catch him

    B.   Take down the names and addresses of any witnesses to the incident

C. Give first aid to the caseworker, if you can, and immediately call for an ambulance
D. Search the people standing around in the room for the knife

19. As a special officer (security officer), you have been patrolling a special section of a hos- 19.____
pital building for a week. Smoking is not allowed in this section because the oxygen tanks
in use here could easily explode. However, you have observed that some employees
sneak into the linen-supply room in this section in order to smoke without anybody see-
ing them.
Of the following, which is the BEST way for you to deal with this situation?

A. Whenever you catch anyone smoking, call his supervisor immediately
B. Request the Building Superintendent to put a padlock on the door of the linen-sup-
ply room
C. Ignore the smoking because you do not want to get a reputation for interfering in
the private affairs of other employees
D. Report the situation to your supervisor and follow his instructions

20. You are on duty at a hospital. You have been assigned to guard the main door, and you 20.____
are responsible for remaining at your post until relieved. On one of the wards for which
you are not responsible, there is a patient who was wounded in a street fight. This patient
is under arrest for killing another man in this fight, and he is supposed to be under round-
the-clock police guard. A nurse tells you that one of the police officers assigned to guard
the patient has suddenly taken ill and has to periodically leave his post to go to the washroom. The nurse is worried because she thinks the patient might try to escape.
Of the following, which is the BEST action for you to take?

A. Tell the nurse to call you whenever the police officer leaves his post so that you can
keep an eye on the patient while the officer is gone
B. Assume that the police officer probably knows his job, and that there is no reason
for you to worry
C. Alert your supervisor to the nurse's report
D. Warn the police officer that the nurse has been talking about him

21. You are on night duty at a hospital where you are responsible for patrolling a large sec- 21.____
tion of the main building. Your supervisor tells you that there have been several nighttime
thefts from a supply room in your section and asks you to be especially alert for suspicious activity near this supply room.
Of the following, which is the MOST reasonable way to carry out your supervisor's
direction?

A. Check the supply room regularly at half-hour intervals
B. Make frequent checks of the supply room at irregular intervals
C. Station yourself by the door of the supply room and stay at this post all night
D. Find a hidden spot from which you can watch the supply room and stay there all
night

22. You are on duty at a vehicle entrance to a hospital. Parking space on the hospital 22.____
grounds is strictly limited, and no one is ever allowed to park there unless they have an
official parking permit. You have just stopped a driver who does not have a parking permit, but he explains that
he is a doctor and he has a patient in the hospital. What should you do?

A. Let him park since he has explained that he is a doctor
B. Ask in a friendly way, *"Can I check your identification?"*
C. Call the Information Desk to make sure there is such a patient in the hospital
D. Tell the driver politely but firmly that he will have to park somewhere else

23. You are on duty at a public building. A man was just mugged on a stairway. The mugger took the man's wallet and started to run down the stairs but tripped and fell. Now the mugger is lying unconscious at the bottom of the stairs and bleeding from the mouth. The FIRST thing you should do is to 23._____

A. search him to see if he is carrying any other stolen property
B. pick him up and carry him away from the stairs
C. try and revive him for questioning
D. put in a call for an ambulance and police assistance

24. After someone breaks into an employee's locker at a public building, you interview the employee to determine what is missing from the locker. The employee becomes hysterical and asks why you are *wasting time with all these questions* instead of going after the thief.
The MOST reasonable thing for you to do is 24._____

A. tell the employee that it is very important to have an accurate description of the missing articles
B. quietly tell the employee to calm down and stop interfering with your work
C. explain to the employee that you are only doing what you were told to do and that you don't make the rules
D. assure the employee that there are a lot of people working on the case and that someone else is probably arresting the thief right now

25. You are on duty at a public building. An employee reports that a man has just held her up and taken her money. The employee says that the man was about 25 years old, with short blond hair and a pale complexion and was wearing blue jeans.
Of the following additional facts, which one would probably be MOST valuable to officers searching the building for the suspect? 25._____

A. The man was wearing dark glasses.
B. He had on a green jacket.
C. He was about 5 feet 8 inches tall.
D. His hands and fingernails were very dirty.

26. When the fire alarm goes off, it is your job as a special officer (security officer) to see that all employees leave the building quickly by the correct exits. A fire alarm has just sounded, and you are checking the offices on one of the floors. A supervisor in one office tells you, *"This is probably just another fire drill. I've sent my office staff out, but I don't want to stop my own work."*
What should you do? 26._____

A. Insist politely but firmly that the supervisor must obey the fire rules.
B. Tell the supervisor that it is all right this time but that the rules must be followed in the future.
C. Tell the supervisor that he is under arrest.
D. Allow the supervisor to do as he sees fit since he is in charge of his own office.

27. You are on duty on the main floor of a public building. You have been informed that a   27.____
briefcase has just been stolen from an office on the tenth floor. You see a man getting off
the elevator with a briefcase that matches the description of the one that was stolen.
What is the FIRST action you should take?

    A. Arrest the man and take him to the nearest public station
    B. Stop the man and say politely that you want to take a look at the briefcase
    C. Take the briefcase from the man and tell him that he cannot have it back unless he
       can prove that it is his
    D. Do not stop the man but note down his description and the exact time he got off the
       elevator

28. You are on duty at a welfare center. You have been told that two clients are arguing with   28.____
a caseworker and making loud threats. You go to the scene, but the caseworker tells you
that everything is now under control. The two clients, who are both mean-looking charac-
ters, are still there but seem to be acting normally.
What SHOULD you do?

    A. Apologize for having made a mistake and go away.
    B. Arrest the two men for having caused a disturbance.
    C. Insist on standing by until the interview is over, then escort the two men from the
       building.
    D. Leave the immediate scene but watch for any further developments.

29. You are on duty at a welfare center. A client comes up to you and says that two men just   29.____
threatened him with a knife and made him give them his money. The client has alcohol
on his breath and he is shabbily dressed. He points out the two men he says took the
money.
Of the following, which is the BEST action to take?

    A. Arrest the two men on the client's complaint.
    B. Ignore the client's complaint since he doesn't look as if he could have had any
       money.
    C. Suggest to the client that he may be imagining things.
    D. Investigate and find out what happened.

Questions 30-35.

DIRECTIONS: Answer Questions 30 through 35 on the basis of the information given in the
                 passage below. Assume that all questions refer to the same state described in
                 the passage.

*The courts and the police consider an "offense" as any conduct that is punishable by a
fine or imprisonment. Such offenses include many kinds of acts - from behavior that is merely
annoying, like throwing a noisy party that keeps everyone awake, all the way up to violent
acts like murder. The law classifies offenses according to the penalties that are provided for
them. In one state, minor offenses are called "violations." A violation is punishable by a fine of
not more than $250 or imprisonment of not more than. 15 days, or both. The annoying behav-
ior mentioned above is an example of a violation. More serious offenses are classified as
"crimes." Crimes are classified by the kind of penalty that is provided. A "misdemeanor" is a
crime that is punishable by a fine of not more than $1,000 or by imprisonment of not more
than one year, or both. Examples of misdemeanors include stealing something with a value*

of $100 or less, turning in a false alarm, or illegally possessing less than 1/8 of an ounce of a dangerous drug. A "felony" is a criminal offense punishable by imprisonment of more than one year. Murder is clearly a felony.

30. According to the above passage, any act that is punishable by imprisonment or by a fine is called a(n)   30.____

    A. offense   B. violation   C. crime   D. felony

31. According to the above passage, which of the following is classified as a crime?   31.____

    A. Offense punishable by 15 days imprisonment
    B. Minor offense
    C. Violation
    D. Misdemeanor

32. According to the above passage, if a person guilty of burglary can receive a prison sentence of 7 years or more, burglary would be classified as a   32.____

    A. violation   B. misdemeanor
    C. felony   D. violent act

33. According to the above passage, two offenses that would BOTH be classified as misdemeanors are   33.____

    A. making unreasonable noise and stealing a $90 bicycle
    B. stealing a $75 radio and possessing 1/16 of an ounce of heroin
    C. holding up a bank and possessing 1/4 of a pound of marijuana
    D. falsely reporting a fire and illegally double-parking

34. The above passage says that offenses are classified according to the penalties provided for them.   34.____
On the basis of clues in the passage, who probably decides what the maximum penalties should be for the different kinds of offenses?

    A. The State lawmakers   B. The City police
    C. The Mayor   D. Officials in Washington, B.C.

35. Of the following, which BEST describes the subject matter of the passage?   35.____

    A. How society deals with criminals
    B. How offenses are classified
    C. Three types of criminal behavior
    D. The police approach to offenders

KEY (CORRECT ANSWERS)

1.	C		16.	B
2.	C		17.	B
3.	B		18.	C
4.	D		19.	D
5.	B		20.	C
6.	A		21.	B
7.	B		22.	D
8.	D		23.	D
9.	C		24.	A
10.	C		25.	C
11.	A		26.	A
12.	D		27.	B
13.	A		28.	D
14.	C		29.	D
15.	B		30.	A

31.	D
32.	C
33.	B
34.	A
35.	B

TEST 2

DIRECTIONS: Each question or incomplete statement is followed by several suggested answers or completions. Select the one that BEST answers the question or completes the statement. *PRINT THE LETTER OF THE CORRECT ANSWER IN THE SPACE AT THE RIGHT.*

Questions 1-5.

DIRECTIONS: Questions 1 through 5 are based on the drawing below showing a view of a waiting area in a public building.

1. A desk is shown in the drawing. Which of the following is on the desk? A(n)   1.____

    A. plant   B. telephone
    C. In-Out file   D. *Information* sign

2. On which floor is the waiting area?   2.____

    A. Basement   B. Main floor
    C. Second floor   D. Third floor

3. The door IMMEDIATELY TO THE RIGHT of the desk is a(n)   3.____

    A. door to the Personnel Office
    B. elevator door
    C. door to another corridor
    D. door to the stairs

4. Among the magazines on the tables in the waiting area are   4.____

    A. TIME and NEWSWEEK
    B. READER'S DIGEST and T.V. GUIDE
    C. NEW YORK and READER'S DIGEST
    D. TIME and T.V. GUIDE

5. One door is partly open. This is the door to   5.____

    A. the Director's office
    B. the Personnel Manager's office
    C. the stairs
    D. an unmarked office

Questions 6-9.

DIRECTIONS: Questions 6 through 9 are based on the drawing below showing the contents
               of a male suspect's pockets.

CONTENTS OF A MALE SUSPECT'S POCKETS

6. The suspect had a slip in his pockets showing an appointment at an out-patient clinic on   6.____

    A. February 9, 2013   B. September 2, 2013
    C. February 19, 2013   D. September 12, 2013

7. The MP3 player that was found on the suspect was made by   7.____

    A. RCA   B. GE   C. Sony   D. Zenith

8. The coins found in the suspect's pockets have a TOTAL value of   8.____

    A. 56¢   B. 77¢   C. $1.05   D. $1.26

9. All except one of the following were found in the suspect's pockets.   9.____
   Which was NOT found? A

    A. ticket stub   B. comb
    C. subway fare   D. pen

Questions 10-18

DIRECTIONS: In answering Questions 10 through 18, assume that *you* means a special officer (security officer) on duty. Your basic responsibilities are safeguarding people and property and maintaining order in the area to which you are assigned. You are in uniform, and you are not armed. You keep in touch with your supervisory station either by telephone or by a two-way radio (a walkie-talkie).

10. You are on duty at a center run by the Department of Social Services. Two teenaged   10.____
boys are on their way out of the center. As they go past you, they look at you and laugh, and one makes a remark to you in Spanish. You do not understand Spanish, but you suspect it was a nasty remark.
What SHOULD you do?

    A. Give the boys a lecture about showing respect for a uniform.
    B. Tell the boys that they had better stay away from the center from now on.
    C. Call for an interpreter and insist that the boy repeat the remark to the interpreter.
    D. Let the boys go on their way since they have done nothing requiring your intervention.

11. You are on duty at a shelter run by the Department of Social Services. You know that   11.____
many of the shelter clients have drinking problems, drug problems, or mental health problems. You get a call for assistance from a caseworker who says a fight has broken out. When you arrive on the scene, you see that about a dozen clients are engaged in a free-for-all and that two or three of them have pulled knives.
The BEST course of action is to

    A. call for additional assistance and order all bystanders away from the area
    B. jump into the center of the fighting group and try to separate the fighters
    C. pick up a heavy object and start swinging at anybody who has a knife
    D. try to find out what clients started the fight and place them under arrest

12. You have been assigned to duty at a children's shelter run by the Department of Social Services. The children range in age from 6 to 15, and many of them are at the shelter because they have no homes to go to.
Of the following, which is the BEST attitude for you to take in dealing with these youngsters?

    A. Assume that they admire and respect anyone in uniform and that they will not usually give you much trouble
    B. Assume that they fear and distrust anyone in uniform and that they are going to give you a hard time unless you act tough
    C. Expect that many of them are going to become juvenile delinquents because of their bad backgrounds and that you should be suspicious of everything they do
    D. Expect that many of them may be emotionally upset and that you should be alert for unusual behavior

12._____

13. You are on duty outside the emergency room of a hospital. You notice that an old man has been sitting on a bench outside the room for a long time. He arrived alone, and he has not spoken to anyone at all.
What SHOULD you do?

    A. Pay no attention to him since he is not bothering anyone.
    B. Tell him to leave since he does not seem to have any business there.
    C. Ask him if you can help him in any way.
    D. Do not speak to him, but keep an eye on him.

13._____

14. You are patrolling a section of a public building. An elderly woman carrying a heavy shopping bag asks you if you would watch the shopping bag for her while she keeps an appointment in the building.
What SHOULD you do?

    A. Watch the shopping bag for her since her appointment probably will not take long.
    B. Refuse her request, explaining that your duties keep you on the move.
    C. Agree to her request just to be polite, but then continue your patrol after the woman is out of sight.
    D. Find a bystander who will agree to watch the shopping bag for her.

14._____

15. You are on duty at a public building. It is nearly 6:00 P.M., and most employees have left for the day.
You see two well-dressed men carrying an office calculating machine out of the building. You SHOULD

    A. stop them and ask for an explanation
    B. follow them to see where they are going
    C. order them to put down the machine and leave the building immediately
    D. take no action since they do not look like burglars

15._____

16. You are on duty patrolling a public building. You have just tripped on the stairs and turned your ankle. The ankle hurts and is starting to swell.
What is the BEST thing to do?

16._____

A. Take a taxi to a hospital emergency room, and from there have a hospital employee call your supervisor to explain the situation.

B. First try soaking your foot in cold water for half an hour, then go off duty if you really cannot walk at all.

C. Report the situation to your supervisor, explaining that you need prompt medical attention for your ankle.

D. Find a place where you can sit until you are due to go off duty, then have a doctor look at your ankle.

17. One of your duties as a special officer (security officer) on night patrol in a public building is to check the washrooms to see that the taps are turned off and that there are no plumbing leaks.
Of the following possible reasons for this inspection, which is probably the MOST important reason?

    17._____

A. If the floor gets wet, someone might slip and fall the next morning.

B. A running water tap might be a sign that there is an intruder in the building.

C. A washroom flood could leak through the ceilings and walls below and cause a lot of damage.

D. Leaks must be reported quickly so that repairs can be scheduled as soon as possible.

18. You are on duty at a public building. A department supervisor tells you that someone has left a suspicious-looking package in the hallway on his floor. You investigate, and you hear ticking in the parcel. You think it could be a bomb.
The FIRST thing you should do is to

    18._____

A. rapidly question employees on this floor to get a description of the person who left the package

B. write down the description of the package and the name of the department supervisor

C. notify your security headquarters that there may be a bomb in the building and that all personnel should be evacuated

D. pick up the package carefully and remove it from the building as quickly as you can

Questions 19-22.

DIRECTIONS: Answer Questions 19 through 22 on the basis of the Fact Situation and the Report of Arrest form below. Questions 19 through 22 ask how the report form should be filled in based on the information given in the Fact Situation.

FACT SITUATION

Jesse Stein is a special officer (security officer) who is assigned to a welfare center at 435 East Smythe Street, Brooklyn. He was on duty there Thursday morning, February 1. At 10:30 A.M., a client named Jo Ann Jones, 40 years old, arrived with her ten-year-old son, Peter. Another client, Mary Alice Wiell, 45 years old, immediately began to insult Mrs. Jones. When Mrs. Jones told her to "go away," Mrs. Wiell pulled out a long knife. The special officer (security officer) intervened and requested Mrs. Wiell to drop the knife. She would not, and he had to use necessary force to disarm her. He arrested her on charges of disorderly conduct, harassment, and possession of a dangerous weapon. Mrs. Wiell lives at 118 Heally Street,

Brooklyn, Apartment 4F, and she is unemployed. The reason for her aggressive behavior is not known.

```
┌─────────────────────────────────────────────────────────────────────────┐
│ REPORT OF ARREST                                                          │
│ 01) _____    (08) _____         │
│     (Prisoner's surname)  (first) (initial)     (Precinct)                │
│ (02) _____    (09) _____         │
│      (Address)                               (Date of arrest)             │
│                                              (Month, Day)                  │
│ (03) _____ (04) _____ (05) _____  (10) _____         │
│      (Date of birth)  (Age)     (Sex)         (Time of arrest)            │
│ (06) _____ (07) _____    (11) _____         │
│      (Occupation)   (Where employed)          (Place of arrest)           │
│─────────────────────────────────────────────────────────────────────────│
│ (12) _____        │
│      (Specific offenses)                                                   │
│─────────────────────────────────────────────────────────────────────────│
│ (13) _____    (14) _____             │
│      (Arresting Officer)                (Officer's No.)                    │
└─────────────────────────────────────────────────────────────────────────┘
```

19. What entry should be made in Blank 01?

    A. Jo Ann Jones B. Jones, Jo Ann
    C. Mary Wiell D. Wiell, Mary A.

20. Which of the following should be entered in Blank 04?

    A. 40 B. 40's C. 45 D. Middle-aged

21. Which of the following should be entered in Blank 09?

    A. Wednesday, February 1, 10:30 A.M.
    B. February 1
    C. Thursday morning, February 2
    D. Morning, February 4

22. Of the following, which would be the BEST entry to make in Blank 11?

    A. Really Street Welfare Center
    B. Brooklyn
    C. 435 E. Smythe St., Brooklyn
    D. 118 Heally St., Apt. 4F

Questions 23-27.

DIRECTIONS: Answer Questions 23 through 27 on the basis of the information given in the Report of Loss or Theft that appears below.

```
┌─────────────────────────────────────────────────────────────────────┐
│ REPORT OF LOSS OR THEFT              Date: 12/4      Time: 9:15 a.m.  │
├─────────────────────────────────────────────────────────────────────┤
│ Complaint made by:  Richard Aldridge        ☐ Owner                  │
│                                                                       │
│                     306 S. Walter St.       ☒ Other - explain:       │
│                                                                       │
│                                             Head of Acctg. Dept.      │
├─────────────────────────────────────────────────────────────────────┤
│ Type of property:  Computer                 Value: $550.00           │
│ Description: Dell                                                     │
│ Location: 768 N Margin Ave., Accounting Dept., 3rd Floor             │
│ Time: Overnight 12/3 - 12/4                                          │
│ Circumstances: Mr. Aldridge reports he arrived at work 8:45 A.M.,    │
│ found office door open and machine missing. Nothing else reported    │
│ missing. I investigated and found signs of forced entry: door lock   │
│ was broken.           Signature of Reporting Officer: B.L. Ramirez   │
├─────────────────────────────────────────────────────────────────────┤
│ Notify:                                                               │
│   ☐ Building & Grounds Office, 768 N. Margin Ave.                    │
│   ☐ Lost Property Office, 110 Brand Ave.                             │
│   ☒ Security Office, 703 N. Wide Street                              │
└─────────────────────────────────────────────────────────────────────┘
```

23. The person who made this complaint is   23.____

   A. a secretary   B. a security officer
   C. Richard Aldridge   D. B.L. Ramirez

24. The report concerns a computer that has been   24.____

   A. lost   B. damaged   C. stolen   D. sold

25. The person who took the computer probably entered the office through   25.____

   A. a door   B. a window   C. the roof   D. the basement

26. When did the head of the Accounting Department first notice that the computer was   26.____
    missing?

   A. December 4 at 9:15 A.M.   B. December 4 at 8:45 A.M.
   C. The night of December 3   D. The night of December 4

27. The event described in the report took place at   27.____

   A. 306 South Walter Street   B. 768 North Margin Avenue
   C. 110 Brand Avenue   D. 703 North Wide Street

Questions 28-33.

DIRECTIONS: Answer Questions 28 through 33 on the basis of the instructions, the code, and the sample question given below.

Assume that a special officer (security officer) at a certain location is equipped with a two-way radio to keep him in constant touch with his security headquarters. Radio messages and replies are given in code form, as follows:

Radio Code for Situation	J	P	M	F	B
Radio Code for Action to be Taken	o	r	a	z	q
Radio Response for Action Being Taken	1	2	3	4	5

Assume that each of the above capital letters is the radio code for a particular type of situation, that the small letter below each capital letter is the radio code for the action a special officer (security officer) is directed to take, and that the number directly below each small letter is the radio response a special officer (security officer) should make to indicate what action was actually taken.

In each of the following Questions 28 through 33, the code letter for the action directed (Column 2) and the code number for the action taken (Column 3) should correspond to the capital letters in Column 1.

If only Column 2 is different from Column 1, mark your answer A.

If only Column 3 is different from Column 1, mark your answer B.

If both Column 2 and Column 3 are different from Column 1, mark your answer C.

If both Columns 2 and 3 are the same as Column 1, mark your answer D.

SAMPLE QUESTION

Column I	Column 2	Column 3
JPFMB	orzaq	12453

The code letters in Column 2 are correct, but the numbers 53 in Column 3 should be 35. Therefore, the answer is B.

	Column 1	Column 2	Column 3	
28.	PBFJM	rqzoa	25413	28.____
29.	MPFBJ	zrqao	32541	29.____
30.	JBFPM	oqzra	15432	30.____
31.	BJPMF	qaroz	51234	31.____
32.	PJFMB	rozaq	21435	32.____
33.	FJBMP	zoqra	41532	33.____

Questions 34-40.

DIRECTIONS: Questions 34 through 40 are based on the instructions given below. Study the instructions and the sample question; then answer Questions 34 through 40 on the basis of this information

INSTRUCTIONS:

In each of the following Questions 34 through 40, the 3-line name and address in Column 1 is the master-list entry, and the 3-line entry in Column 2 is the information to be checked against the master list.

If there is one line that does not match, mark your answer A.

If there are two lines that do not match, mark your answer B.

If all three lines do not match, mark your answer C.

If the lines all match exactly, mark your answer D.

SAMPLE QUESTION:

Column 1	Column 2
Mark L. Field	Mark L. Field
11-09 Prince Park Blvd.	11-99 Prince Park
Bronx, N.Y. 11402	Bronx, N.Y. 11401

The first lines in each column match exactly. The second lines do not match, since 11-09 does not match 11-99 and Blvd. does not match Way. The third lines do not match either, since 11402 does not match 11401. Therefore, there are two lines that do not match and the correct answer is B.

	Column 1	Column 2	
34.	Jerome A. Jackson	Jerome A. Johnson	34._____
	1243 14th Avenue	1234 14th Avenue	
	New York, N.Y. 10023	New York, N.Y. 10023	
35.	Sophie Strachtheim	Sophie Strachtheim	35._____
	33-28 Connecticut Ave.	33-28 Connecticut Ave.	
	Far Rockaway, N.Y. 11697	Far Rockaway, N.Y. 11697	
36.	Elisabeth N.T. Gorrell	Elizabeth N.T. Gorrell	36._____
	256 Exchange St.	256 Exchange St.	
	New York, N.Y. 10013	New York, N.Y. 10013	
37.	Maria J. Gonzalez	Maria J. Gonzalez	37._____
	7516 E. Sheepshead Rd.	7516 N. Shepshead Rd.	
	Brooklyn, N.Y. 11240	Brooklyn, N.Y. 11240	
38.	Leslie B. Brautenweiler	Leslie B. Brautenwieler	38._____
	21 57A Seller Terr.	21-75A Seiler Terr.	
	Flushing, N.Y. 11367	Flushing, N.J. 11367	

39. Rigoberto J. Peredes
    157 Twin Towers, #18F
    Tottenville, S.I., N.Y.

    Rigoberto J. Peredes
    157 Twin Towers, #18F
    Tottenville, S.I., N.Y.

    39.____

40. Pietro F. Albino
    P.O. Box 7548
    Floral Park, N.Y. 11005

    Pietro F. Albina
    P.O. Box 7458
    Floral Park, N.Y. 11005

    40.____

KEY (CORRECT ANSWERS)

1.	D	11.	A	21.	B	31.	A
2.	C	12.	D	22.	C	32.	D
3.	B	13.	C	23.	C	33.	A
4.	D	14.	B	24.	C	34.	B
5.	B	15.	A	25.	A	35.	D
6.	A	16.	C	26.	B	36.	A
7.	C	17.	C	27.	B	37.	A
8.	D	18.	C	28.	D	38.	C
9.	D	19.	D	29.	C	39.	D
10.	D	20.	C	30.	B	40.	B

EXAMINATION SECTION
TEST 1

DIRECTIONS: Each question or incomplete statement is followed by several suggested answers or completions. Select the one that BEST answers the question or completes the statement. *PRINT THE LETTER OF THE CORRECT ANSWER IN THE SPACE AT THE RIGHT.*

Questions 1-9.

DIRECTIONS: Questions 1 through 9 are to be answered SOLELY on the basis of the following information and the DIRECTORY OF SERVICES.

Officer Johnson has just been assigned to the North End Service Facility and is now on his post in the main lobby. The facility is open to the public from 9 A.M. to 5 P.M. each Monday through Friday, except on Thursdays when it is open from 9 A.M. to 7 P.M. The facility is closed on holidays.

Officer Johnson must ensure an orderly flow of visitors through the lobby of the facility. To accomplish this, Officer Johnson gives directions and provides routine information to clients and other members of the public who enter and leave the facility through the lobby.

In order to give directions and provide routine information to visitors, such as information concerning the location of services, Officer Johnson consults the Directory of Services shown below. Officer Johnson must ensure that clients are directed to the correct room for service and are sent to that room only during the hours that the particular service is available. When clients ask for the location of more than one service, they should be directed to go first to the service that will close soonest.

NORTH END SERVICE FACILITY
DIRECTORY OF SERVICES

Room	Type of Service	Days Available	Hours Open
101	Facility Receptionist	Monday, Tuesday, Wednesday, Friday	9 AM- 5 PM
		Thursday	9 AM- 7 PM
103	Photo Identification Cards	Monday, Wednesday, Friday	9 AM-12 Noon
104	Lost and Stolen Identification Cards	Wednesday, Thursday	9 AM-5 PM
105	Applications for Welfare/Food Stamps	Wednesday, Friday	1 PM-5 PM
107	Recertification for Welfare/Food Stamps	Monday, Thursday	10 AM- 12 Noon
108	Medicaid Applications	Tuesday, Wednesday	2 PM-5 PM
109	Medicaid Complaints	Tuesday, Wednesday	10 AM-2 PM
110, 111	Social Worker	Monday, Wednesday	9 AM-12 Noon
		Tuesday, Friday	1 PM-5 PM
		Thursday	9 AM- 5 PM
114	Hearing Room (By appointment only)	Monday, Thursday	9 AM-5 PM

DIRECTORY OF SERVICES
(CONT'D)

Room	Type of Service	Days Available	Hours Open
115	Hearing Information	Monday, Tuesday, Wednesday, Thursday, Friday	9 AM-1 PM
206, 207	Nutrition Aid	Monday, Wednesday, Friday	10 AM-2 PM
		Tuesday, Thursday	9 AM-12 Noon
215	Health Clinic	Monday, Tuesday, Wednesday, Friday	9 AM-5 PM
		Thursday	9 AM-7 PM
220	Facility Administrative Office	Monday, Tuesday, Wednesday, Thursday, Friday	9 AM-5 PM

1. It is Tuesday morning and Ms. Loretta Rogers, a client of the North End Service Facility, asks Officer Johnson where she should go in order to apply for Medicaid. Officer Johnson tells Ms. Rogers to go to Room _____ at _____.

    A. 108; 1:00 P.M.
    B. 109; 11:00 A.M.
    C. 108; 2:00 P.M.
    D. 109; 2:00 P.M.

2. On Friday at 11:00 A.M., Mrs. Ruth Ramos, a new client at the North End Service Facility, tells Officer Johnson that she wants to obtain a photo identification card and see a social worker.
   Officer Johnson should direct Mrs. Ramos to first go to Room

    A. 103   B. 104   C. 110   D. 220

3. On Friday at 10:30 A.M., a client at the North End Service Facility who is directed by Officer Johnson to go to Room 206 will be able to receive service regarding

    A. Recertification for Welfare/Food Stamps
    B. Hearing Information
    C. Medicaid Applications
    D. Nutrition Aid

4. At 9:00 A.M. on Monday, a client at the North End Service Facility who is directed by Officer Johnson to Room 101 for service will find

    A. Nutrition Aid
    B. Facility Receptionist
    C. Health Clinic
    D. Hearing Information

5. On Tuesday at 12:30 P.M., Mr. Paul Brown tells Officer Johnson that he lost his identification card and wants to obtain a new one as soon as possible.
   Officer Johnson should direct Mr. Brown to go to Room 104

    A. immediately
    B. at 1:00 P.M. that day
    C. at 9:00 A.M. on Wednesday
    D. at 2:00 P.M. on Friday

6. A client at the North End Service Facility explains to Officer Johnson that he wants to   6.____
   make an appointment with a Social Worker.
   The client should be directed to go to Room

   A. 104   B. 110   C. 115   D. 215

7. Ms. Alice Lee is a client at the North End Service Facility who has a 10:00 A.M. appoint-   7.____
   ment on Thursday in the Hearing Room and does not know where to go.
   Officer Johnson should direct Ms. Lee to go to Room

   A. 101   B. 110   C. 112   D. 114

8. Officer Johnson is asked by a visitor which services are available on Thursdays between   8.____
   5:00 P.M. and 7:00 P.M. Officer Johnson should inform the visitor that an available service during that time is

   A. Health Clinic   B. Medicaid Complaints
   C. Nutrition Aid   D. Social Worker

9. Mr. Jack Klein, a visitor to the North End Service Facility, asks Officer Johnson when and   9.____
   where he can file a complaint concerning Medicaid.
   Officer Johnson should inform Mr. Klein that he may go to Room

   A. 108 on Tuesday or Wednesday between 2:00 P.M. and 5:00 P.M.
   B. 109 on Tuesday or Wednesday between 10:00 A.M. and 2:00 P.M.
   C. 115 on Monday or Tuesday between 10:00 A.M. and 12:00 Noon
   D. 215 on Thursday between 9:00 A.M. and 7:00 P.M.

Questions 10-12.

DIRECTIONS: Questions 10 through 12 are to be answered SOLELY on the basis of the fol-
               lowing information.

Security Officers should act in accordance with guidelines included in a manual provided
to security staff. Assume that the following guidelines apply to Officers when in contact with
visitors or clients in a facility:

   1. Try to see things from the visitor's or client's point of view.
   2. Ignore insulting comments.
   3. Maintain a calm and patient manner.
   4. Speak quietly, courteously, and tactfully.

10. Officer Renee Williams is patrolling the lobby area of her facility when she hears a client   10.____
    angrily yelling at the receptionist. She goes to investigate the situation and finds out from
    the receptionist that the client is one hour late for his appointment with a social worker
    who now has other appointments. The client demands to be seen by the social worker
    immediately. Officer Williams angrily tells the client that it is his own fault that he missed
    his appointment and he should stop bothering the receptionist and go home.
    In this situation, Officer Williams' behavior towards the client is

    A. *proper,* chiefly because it is the client's fault that he missed his appointment
    B. *improper,* chiefly because security officers should stay calm and speak courteously
       when dealing with clients
    C. *proper,* chiefly because the client had yelled at the receptionist
    D. *improper,* chiefly because the security officer should have ignored the whole incident

11. During his tour, Officer Montgomery is passing through his facility's waiting room on the way to the cafeteria for a break. As Officer Montgomery passes by a visitor, the visitor mutters an insulting remark about the Officer's appearance. Officer Montgomery ignores the visitor and the remark and proceeds on his way to the cafeteria.
Officer Montgomery's action in this situation is

    A. *correct,* chiefly because it is not necessary for Officer Montgomery to respond to visitors while on a break
    B. *incorrect,* chiefly because Officer Montgomery should have ejected the visitor from the facility
    C. *correct,* chiefly because special officers should ignore insults
    D. *incorrect,* chiefly because visitors should not be allowed to ridicule authority figures such as special officers

11.____

12. While patrolling the facility parking lot, Officer Klausner sees an unoccupied car parked in front of a fire hydrant. Officer Klausner writes out a summons for a parking violation and places it on the windshield of the car. As the Officer begins to walk away, the owner of the car spots the summons on the windshield and runs over to the car. The car owner is furious at getting the summons, confronts the Officer, and curses him loudly.
In this situation, Officer Klausner should

    A. curse back at the car owner just as loudly
    B. push him out of the way and resume patrol
    C. calmly explain to him the nature of the violation
    D. return all the insults but in a calm tone

12.____

Question 13.

DIRECTIONS: Question 13 is to be answered SOLELY on the basis of the following information.

Special Officers are permitted to give only general information about social services. They shall not provide advice concerning specific procedures.

13. Special Officer Lynn King is on post near the Medicaid Office in the Manhattan Income Maintenance Center. While Officer King is on post, a client approaches her and asks which forms must be filled out in order to apply for Medicaid benefits. Officer King tells the client that she cannot help him and directs the client to the Medicaid Office.
In this situation, Officer King's response to the client's question is

    A. *correct,* chiefly because Officer King's duties do not include providing any information to clients
    B. *incorrect,* chiefly because Officer King should have provided as much specific information as possible to the client
    C. *correct,* chiefly because Officer King may not advise clients on social services procedures
    D. *incorrect,* chiefly because Officer King should know which forms are used in the facility

13.____

Question 14.

DIRECTIONS: Question 14 is to be answered SOLELY on the basis of the following information.

Security Officers must request that visitors and clients show identification and inspect that identification before allowing them to enter restricted areas in the facility.

14.   Security Officer Crane is assigned to a fixed post outside Commissioner Maxwell's office, which is a restricted area. A visitor approaches Officer Crane's desk and states that he is Robert Maxwell and has an appointment with the Commissioner, who is his brother. Officer Crane checks the appointment book, verifies that Robert Maxwell has an appointment with the Commissioner, and allows the visitor to enter the office.
In this situation, Officer Crane's action in allowing the visitor admittance to the Commissioner's office is

14.____

   A.   *correct,* chiefly because he verified that Robert Maxwell had an appointment with the Commissioner
   B.   *incorrect,* chiefly because all visitors must show identification before entering restricted areas
   C.   *correct,* chiefly because it would insult the Commissioner's brother if he was asked to show identification
   D.   *incorrect,* chiefly because he should have called the Commissioner to verify that he has a brother

Question 15.

DIRECTIONS: Question 15 is to be answered SOLELY on the basis of the following information.

While on duty, a Special Officer must give his rank, name, and shield number to any person who requests it.

15.   Special Officer Karen Mitchell is assigned to patrol an area in the North Bronx Service Facility. While on patrol, Officer Mitchell observes a visitor asking other clients in the lobby for money. Upon investigation, she determines that the visitor has no official business in the facility and asks the visitor to leave the premises. The individual says that he will leave but demands to know Officer Mitchell's name and shield number.
In response to the visitor's demand, Officer Mitchell should

15.____

   A.   give the individual her name and shield number
   B.   inform him that he can only obtain that information from her supervisor
   C.   ignore his demand and resume her patrol
   D.   tell the visitor that she will issue a summons to him if he keeps bothering her

Question 16.

DIRECTIONS: Question 16 is to be answered SOLELY on the basis of the following information.

A member of the Security Staff must follow guidelines for providing information to reporters concerning official facility business. Special Officers shall not be interviewed, nor make public speeches or statements pertaining to official business unless authorized. Security Staff must receive authorization from the Office of Public Affairs before speaking to reporters on any matters pertaining to official facility business.

16. You are a Special Officer in a Men's Shelter. A reporter approaches you as you are leaving the building. The reporter requests that you give an insider's view on conditions in the shelter. He assures you that you will remain anonymous.
You should tell the reporter that you

16.____

   A. must obtain permission from your immediate supervisor before giving any interviews
   B. will be more than happy to provide him with information concerning conditions in the shelter
   C. must receive authorization from the Office of Public Affairs before giving any interviews
   D. may not give him any information, but that your supervisor will be able to provide him with the requested information.

Questions 17-21.

DIRECTIONS: Questions 17 through 21 are to be answered SOLELY on the basis of the following information.

During their tours, Security Officers are required to transmit and receive information and commands over two-way portable radios from other security staff members. Officers use a numbered code to transmit information over the radio. For example, an officer who calls *10-13* into his radio communicates to other officers and supervisors that he is in need of assistance. Assume that the code numbers shown below along with their specified meanings are those used by Special Officers.

Code	Meaning
10-01	Call your command
10-02	Report to your command
10-03	Call Dispatcher
10-04	Acknowledgment
10-05	Repeat message
10-06	Stand-by
10-07	Verify
10-08	Respond to specified area and advise
10-10	Investigate
10-13	Officer needs help
10-20	Robbery in progress
10-21	Burglary in progress
10-22	Larceny in progress
10-24	Assault in progress
10-30	Robbery has occurred

10-31	Burglary has occurred
10-34	Assault has occurred
10-40	Unusual incident
10-41	Vehicle accident
10-42	Traffic or parking problem
10-43	Electrical problem
10-50	Dispute or noise
10-52	Disorderly person/group
10-60	Ambulance needed
10-61	Police Department assistance required
10-64	Fire alarm
10-70	Arrived at scene
10-71	Arrest
10-72	Unfounded
10-73	Condition corrected
10-74	Resuming normal duties

17. Officer Cramer is patrolling Parking Lot A when he receives a radio message from Sergeant Wong. Sergeant Wong directs Officer Cramer to respond to Parking Lot B to investigate a reported traffic problem. Upon arriving at Parking Lot B, Officer Cramer observes a vehicle blocking a loading dock so that a delivery truck cannot gain access to the dock. After notification is made to the owner of the vehicle, the vehicle is moved, allowing the delivery truck to gain access to the loading dock. Which of the following should Officer Cramer use to BEST report the events that occurred back to Sergeant Wong?   17.____

   A. 10-72,10-41,10-73   B. 10-70,10-42,10-73
   C. 10-70, 10-41, 10-74   D. 10-72, 10-42,10-74

18. Officer Garret receives a message of *10-24, 10-10* on his radio from his supervisor, Sergeant Gomez. Officer Garret responds to the scene and later sends Sergeant Gomez the following message in response: *10-70, 10-72, 10-74*. Which of the following events are reported by use of those codes?   18.____
   Sergeant Gomez ordered Officer Garret to investigate an assault

   A. in progress. Officer Garret arrived at the scene, discovered that the report was unfounded, and resumed normal duties.
   B. that had occurred. Officer Garret arrived at the scene, made an arrest, and then resumed normal duties.
   C. that had occurred. Officer Garret arrived at the scene and discovered that the report was unfounded and resumed normal duties.
   D. in progress. Officer Garret arrived at the scene, made an arrest, and then resumed normal duties.

19. Officer Torres is patrolling the grounds of his facility when he receives a radio message   19._____
from Sergeant Washington. In response to the radio message, Officer Torres goes to the
facility's parking lot and issues a summons to a vehicle blocking an ambulance entrance.
The radio message that Officer Torres received from Sergeant Washington is 10-10,

    A. 10-21   B. 10-40   C. 10-42   D. 10-43

20. Officer Oxford transmits the following codes by radio to Sergeant Joseph: *10-20, 10-13*.   20._____
The response that Officer Oxford receives from Sergeant Joseph on her radio is *10-04*.
Which one of the following events are reported by the use of those codes?
Officer Oxford informed Sergeant Joseph that

    A. a robbery was in progress and that she needs assistance, and Sergeant Joseph
acknowledged her message
    B. an assault was in progress and that she wants him to respond to the area, and Sergeant Joseph acknowledged her message
    C. a burglary was in progress and that someone must investigate, and Sergeant
Joseph responded that he is standing by
    D. a larceny was in progress and that she needs him to call a dispatcher. Sergeant
Joseph reports this incident to his command.

21. While on patrol, Officer Robinson observes that the hall lights in Wing *B* are flickering on   21._____
and off. Officer Robinson calls the Maintenance Office and a maintenance worker
responds and corrects the problem.
The radio code that Officer Robinson should transmit to his supervisor to report this
incident is

    A. 10-06,10-08   B. 10-40,10-64
    C. 10-43,10-73   D. 10-61,10-07

Question 22.

DIRECTIONS: Question 22 is to be answered SOLELY on the basis of the following information.

The two-way portable radios used by Security or Special Officers to communicate with
other security staff members are to be used for official business only. In addition, when transmitting official business, transmission time (time spent transmitting information to other staff)
should be kept to a minimum.

22. During his tour, Special Officer Banks calls Sergeant Gates in the patrolroom over the   22._____
radio and asks if his wife, Alice Banks, had telephoned. Sergeant Gates tells Officer
Banks that his wife has not called. Officer Banks then requests that Sergeant Gates
notify him as soon as his wife calls because he is expecting an important message concerning his family.
In this situation, Officer Banks' use of his radio is

    A. *appropriate*, chiefly because his transmission time was not excessive
    B. *inappropriate*, chiefly because he should have made the transmission on his break
    C. *appropriate*, chiefly because his transmission concerned an important family matter
    D. *inappropriate*, chiefly because radios are to be used for official business only

Question 23.

DIRECTIONS: Question 23 is to be answered SOLELY on the basis of the following informa-
                        tion.

Special Officers are responsible for monitoring and responding to radio messages, even
if the officer is on meal break, performing clerical duties, or away from his post for other rea
sons. An officer shall answer radio messages directed to him during his tour.

23.   Officer Lewis is chatting with friends in the cafeteria while on her scheduled meal break   23._____
        when she receives a radio message from Sergeant Baker. Sergeant Baker informs
        Officer Lewis that trouble has broken out at Location A and directs her to report to Loca-
        tion A immediately to assist the officers on the scene. Officer Lewis leaves the cafeteria
        immediately and reports to the scene.
        Officer Lewis' action in response to Sergeant Baker's radio message is

        A.   *correct,* chiefly because Officer Lewis is responsible for responding to all radio
               messages
        B.   *incorrect,* chiefly because Officer Lewis is on meal break and therefore *off-duty*
        C.   *correct,* chiefly because Officer Lewis was not doing anything important during her
               meal break
        D.   *incorrect,* chiefly because the situation was not declared a *total emergency*

Question 24.

DIRECTIONS: Question 24 is to be answered SOLELY on the basis of the following informa-
                        tion.

Special Officers must immediately report to their supervisor any incident or condition in
the facility that may cause danger or inconvenience to the public.

24.   Special Officer Scott is patrolling a small, crowded waiting room in his facility when two   24._____
        male clients start arguing with each other, shoving chairs around and frightening the
        other clients. Officer Scott intervenes in the argument, issues summonses for Disorderly
        Conduct to the individuals involved in the dispute, and escorts them off the premises.
        Officer Scott then records the incident in his memo book and resumes patrol.
        In this situation, the FIRST action that Officer Scott should have taken when he
        observed the argument start between the two men is to

        A.   call for help from Special Officers on nearby posts to restrain the men who were
               fighting
        B.   report the incident to his supervisor immediately
        C.   attempt to separate the men who were fighting in order to stop the fight
        D.   evacuate the waiting room so that innocent bystanders would not be injured

Question 25.

DIRECTIONS: Question 25 is to be answered SOLELY on the basis of the following information.

An Officer on duty in a facility must remain on post until properly relieved. If not properly relieved as scheduled, he must notify his immediate supervisor by radio of this fact and follow the supervisor's instructions.

25. Officer Clough is working on an 8:00 A.M. to 4:00 P.M. tour. Officer Clough is to be relieved at 4:00 P.M. by Security Officer Crandall, who works the 4:00 P.M. to 12:00 Midnight shift. However, as of 4:15 P.M., Officer Crandall has not appeared to relieve Officer Clough, so Officer Clough leaves his post to find Officer Crandall. In this situation, Officer Clough's action is

    A. *correct,* chiefly because his tour was over and he wanted to go home
    B. *incorrect,* chiefly because he should have notified his supervisor of Officer Crandall's failure to relieve him
    C. *correct,* chiefly because Officer Clough is attempting to locate Officer Crandall so that the post will be covered
    D. *incorrect,* chiefly because Officer Clough should have left his post as soon as his tour ended rather than working any overtime

Questions 26-28.

DIRECTIONS: Questions 26 through 28 are to be answered SOLELY on the basis of the following information.

A summons is a written notice that a person is accused of violating a code or regulation. Special Officers have the authority to issue summonses to individuals for on-premises parking or traffic violations, or violations of the City Administrative Code. Summonses for violations of the Penal Law, such as for Disorderly Conduct, may also be issued.

The following is a list of types of summonses issued for violations and their descriptions:

Type of Summons	Description of Violation
Class A	Parking in fire lanes
Class A	Parking in space reserved for the handicapped
Class A	Vehicle blocking driveway
Class B	Disobeying stop sign
Class C	Disorderly Conduct
Class C	Harassment
Environmental Control Board	Smoking Violations
Environmental Control Board	Public Health Code

26. While on patrol, Special Officer Gladys Jones observes a parked car that is blocking a driveway.
She should issue a summons for a violation which is a

    A. Class A type
    B. Class B type
    C. Class C type
    D. Environmental Control Board

27. ...r in a fire lane, and quickly runs inside the facil- 27. ___
...an is unsuccessful.
...summons that the Special Officer on duty

    B.   Class B
    D.   Environmental Control Board

28 ...serves a visitor smoking a cigarette in an area 28. ___
...on asks the visitor to stop smoking and shows
...tor refuses to comply.
...summons?

    B.   Class B
    D.   Environmental Control Board

Q...
D... ... to be answered SOLELY on the basis of the following information and the Summons Form and Fact Pattern.

Special Officers must complete a summons form by filling in the appropriate information. A completed summons must include the name and address of the accused; license or other identification number; vehicle identification; the section number of the code, regulation, or law violated; a brief description of the violation; any scheduled fine; information about the time and place of occurrence; and the name, rank, and signature of the Special Officer issuing the summons.

The information listed on the Summons Form may or may not be correct.

SUMMONS FORM

	NOTICE OF VIOLATION No. 5 56784989	THE PEOPLE OF THE STATE OF NEW YORK VS._____	

LINE;

Line			
1	OPERATOR PRESENT NO (YES) REFUSED ID		
2	LAST NAME *Tucker*	FIRST NAME *James*	MIDDLE INITIAL *T*
3	STREET ADDRESS *205 E. 53rd Street*		
4	CITY (AS SHOWN ON LICENSE) *Brooklyn, NY 11234*		
5	DRIVER LICENSE OR IDENTIFICATION NO. *J-7156907834*	STATE *NY* CLASS *5*	DATE EXPIRES *1/12/13*
6	SEX *M*	DATE OF BIRTH *1/12/65*	
7	LICENSE PLATE NO. *CVR-632*	STATE *NY* DATE EXPIRES *8/12/12*	OPERATOR OWN VEHICLE? (YES) NO
8	BODY TYPE *Sedan*	MAKE *Dodge*	COLOR *Green*

THE PERSON DESCRIBED ABOVE IS CHARGED AS FOLLOWS:

Line			
9	ISSUE TIME *9:30 A.M.* DATE OF OFFENSE *2/5/12*	TIME FIRST OBSERVED *9:28 A.M.*	COUNTY *Kings*
10	PLACE OF OCCURRENCE *451 Clarkson Ave., Brooklyn, NY*		PRECINCT *71st*
11	IN VIOLATION OF SECTION *81-B*	CODE *40*	LAW *New York State Traffic Regulation*
12	DESCRIPTION OF VIOLATION *Vehicle parked in front of a fire hydrant*		
13	SCHEDULED FINE $10 $15 $20 $25 $30 ($40) Other $____		
14	RANK/NAME OF ISSUING OFFICER *Special Officer Joseph Robbins*	SIGNATURE OF ISSUING OFFICER *Joseph Robbins*	

FACT PATTERN

On February 5, 2012, at 9:28 A.M., Special Officer Joseph Robbins is patrolling the grounds of the Brooklyn Hills Income Maintenance Center, located at 451 Clarkson Ave., Brooklyn, NY, when he observes an unoccupied parked vehicle blocking a fire hydrant near the facility's entrance. As Officer Robbins begins to write up a summons for the violation, James Tucker, the owner of the vehicle, emerges from the facility and comes over. While getting in his car, he asks why he is getting a summons. Officer Robbins explains to Mr. Tucker that he is in violation of traffic regulations pertaining to access to fire hydrants and asks him for identification. Mr. Tucker gives Officer Robbins his driver's license, showing the following information:

Name:	Tucker, James T.
Address:	205 E. 53rd Street, Brooklyn, NY 11234
Date of Birth:	January 12, 1965
Driver's License:	J-7156907894
Driver License Expiration Date:	January 12, 2013
Class:	5

29. The *place of occurrence* of the violation described in the Fact Pattern is on line _____ of the Summons Form.

   A. 2   B. 3   C. 8   D. 10

30. Which one of the following lines on the Summons Form shows information that does NOT agree with information given in the Fact Pattern?

   A. 1   B. 2   C. 4   D. 5

31. Which of the following is the date on which the violation occurred?

   A. 1/12/12   B. 2/5/12   C. 8/12/12   D. 1/12/13

32. Following are two sentences which may or may not be written in correct English:
   I. Two clients assaulted the officer.
   II. The van is illegally parked.
   Which one of the following statements is CORRECT?

   A. Only Sentence I is written in correct English.
   B. Only Sentence II is written in correct English.
   C. Sentences I and II are both written in correct English.
   D. Neither Sentence I nor Sentence II is written in correct English.

33. Following are two sentences which may or may not be written in correct English:
   I. Security Officer Rollo escorted the visitor to the patrolroom.
   II. Two entry were made in the facility logbook.
   Which one of the following statements is CORRECT?

   A. Only Sentence I is written in correct English.
   B. Only Sentence II is written in correct English.
   C. Sentences I and II are both written in correct English.
   D. Neither Sentence I nor Sentence II is written in correct English.

34. Following are two sentences which may or may not be written in correct English: 34.____
    I. Officer McElroy putted out a small fire in the wastepaper basket.
    II. Special Officer Janssen told the visitor where he could obtained a pass.
Which one of the following statements is CORRECT?

   A. Only Sentence I is written in correct English.
   B. Only Sentence II is written in correct English.
   C. Sentences I and II are both written in correct English.
   D. Neither Sentence I nor Sentence II are written in correct English.

35. Following are two sentences which may or may not be written in correct English: 35.____
    I. Security Officer Warren observed a broken window while he was on his post in Hallway *C*.
    II. The worker reported that two typewriters had been stoled from the office.
Which one of the following statements is CORRECT?

   A. Only Sentence I is written in correct English.
   B. Only Sentence II is written in correct English.
   C. Sentences I and II are both written in correct English.
   D. Neither Sentence I nor Sentence II is written in correct English.

KEY (CORRECT ANSWERS)

1.	C		16.	C
2.	A		17.	B
3.	D		18.	A
4.	B		19.	C
5.	C		20.	A
6.	B		21.	C
7.	D		22.	D
8.	A		23.	A
9.	B		24.	B
10.	B		25.	B
11.	C		26.	A
12.	C		27.	A
13.	C		28.	D
14.	B		29.	D
15.	A		30.	D

31.	B
32.	C
33.	A
34.	D
35.	A

TEST 2

DIRECTIONS: Each question or incomplete statement is followed by several suggested answers or completions. Select the one that BEST answers the question or completes the statement. *PRINT THE LETTER OF THE CORRECT ANSWER IN THE SPACE AT THE RIGHT.*

Questions 1-5.

DIRECTIONS: Questions 1 through 5 are to be answered SOLELY on the basis of the following information.

Special Officers have the power to arrest members of the public who commit crimes in violation of the Penal Law. Assume that certain classes of crimes covered by various sections of the Penal Law are described below. Special Officers must be able to apply this information when making an arrest in order to accurately determine the type of crime that has been committed.

Crime	Class of Crime	Description of Crime	Section
Petit Larceny	A Misdemeanor	Stealing property worth up to $250	155.25
Grand Larceny 3rd Degree	E Felony	Stealing property worth more than $250	155.30
Grand Larceny 2nd Degree	D Felony	Stealing property worth more than $1,500	155.35
Grand Larceny 1st Degree	C Felony	Stealing property worth any amount of money while making a person fear injury or damage to property	155.40
Assault 3rd Degree	A Misdemeanor	Injuring a person	120.00
Assault 2nd Degree	D Felony	1. Seriously injuring a person; or 2. Injuring an officer of the law	120.05
Assault 1st Degree	C Felony	Seriously injuring a person using a deadly or dangerous weapon	120.10
Disorderly Conduct	Violation	1. Engages in fighting or threatening behavior; or 2. Makes unreasonable noise	240.20
Robbery 3rd Degree	D Felony	Stealing property by force	160.05
Robbery 2nd Degree	C Felony	1. Stealing property by force with the help of another person; or 2. Stealing property by force and injuring any person	160.10
Robbery 1st Degree	B Felony	Stealing property by force and seriously injuring the owner of property	160.15

1. Which one of the following crimes is considered to be Class *A* Misdemeanor?   1.____

    A. Grand Larceny - 3rd Degree
    B. Grand Larceny - 2nd Degree
    C. Assault - 3rd Degree
    D. Assault - 2nd Degree

2. Which one of the following crimes is considered to be Class *B* Felony?   2.____

    A. Robbery - 2nd Degree
    B. Robbery - 1st Degree
    C. Grand Larceny - 3rd Degree
    D. Grand Larceny - 2nd Degree

3. A worker at a facility reports that a typewriter worth $400 has been stolen from her office.   3.____
   Which one of the following is the type of crime that has been committed?

    A. Grand Larceny - 3rd Degree
    B. Grand Larceny - 2nd Degree
    C. Grand Larceny - 1st Degree
    D. Petit Larceny

4. A visitor at a facility begins yelling very loudly at a receptionist and shakes his fist at her.   4.____
   The visitor refuses to stop yelling when an officer tries to calm him down, and he shakes
   his fist at the officer. Which one of the following is the type of crime that occurred?

    A. Assault - 3rd Degree   B. Assault - 2nd Degree
    C. Assault - 1st Degree   D. Disorderly Conduct

5. An officer has apprehended and arrested a visitor who was attempting to leave the facil-   5.____
   ity with a radio he had stolen from an office. The radio is worth $100.
   Under which one of the following sections of the Penal Law should the visitor be
   charged? Section

    A. 155.25   B. 155.30   C. 155.35   D. 155.40

Questions 6-12.

DIRECTIONS: Questions 6 through 12 are to be answered SOLELY on the basis of the Arrest
              Report Form and Incident Report shown on the following page. These reports
              were submitted by Special Officer John Clark, Shield #512, to his supervisor,
              Sergeant Joseph Lewis, Shield #818, of the North Bay Health Clinic

   Special Officers are required to complete both an Arrest Report Form and an Incident
Report whenever an unusual incident or an arrest occurs. The Arrest Report Form provides
detailed information regarding the victim and the person arrested, along with a brief description of the incident.

   The Incident Report provides a detailed description of the incident. Both reports include
the following information: WHO was involved in the incident, including witnesses; WHAT happened and HOW it happened; WHERE and WHEN the incident occurred; and WHY the incident occurred.

ARREST REPORT FORM

ARREST INFORMATION (1)	TIME OF OCCURRENCE 11:15 A.M.		DATE OF OCCURRENCE February 1, 2012		DAY OF WEEK Monday
INFORMATION ABOUT VICTIM (2)	VICTIM'S NAME Darlene Kirk		ADDRESS 7855 Cruger St., Bronx, NY 10488		
(3)	SEX F	DATE OF BIRTH 9/3/75	RACE White	HOME TELEPHONE # 212-733-3462	SOCIAL SECURITY # 245-63-0772
INFORMATION ABOUT PERSON ARRESTED (4)	NAME OF PERSON ARRESTED Elsie Gardner		ADDRESS 2447 Southern Pkway, Bronx, NY 10467		
(5)	SEX F	DATE OF BIRTH 7/9/80	RACE White	HOME TELEPHONE # 212-513-7029	SOCIAL SECURITY # 244-08-0569
(6)	HEIGHT 5'5"	WEIGHT 135 lbs.	HAIR COLOR Brown	CLOTHING Black coat/red pants	
DESCRIPTION OF CRIME (7)	SECTION OF PENAL LAW 120.00		TYPE OF CRIME Assault - 3rd Degree		
(8)	TIME OF ARREST 11:35 A.M.		DATE OF ARREST 2/1/12	LOCATION OF ARREST 635 Bay Avenue Bronx, NY	
(9)	DESCRIPTION OF INCIDENT The defendant, Elsie Gardner, struck the victim after the victim requested that Ms. Gardner stop smoking in a "NO SMOKING" area. Two witnesses verified the victim's account of the incident.				
INFORMATION ABOUT ARRESTING OFFICER (10)	REPORTING OFFICER'S SIGNATURE *John Clark*			NAME PRINTED John Clark	
(11)	RANK Special Officer		SHIELD NUMBER 512		

INCIDENT REPORT

(1) At 11:15 A.M. on February 1, 2012, I was directed by Sergeant Mark Lewis via two-way radio to report to the Nutrition Clinic on the 4th Floor to investigate a disturbance. (2) Special Officer Anna Colon, Shield #433, was directed to assist me. (3) At 11:16 A.M., Officer Colon and I arrived at the Health Clinic and observed a patient, Elsie Gardner, repeatedly strike Health Clinic receptionist Darlene Kirk about the head and neck. (4) Officer Colon restrained Ms. Gardner while I placed handcuffs on her wrists. (5) Ms. Kirk complained that her neck felt sore. (6) After being examined by Dr. Stone, Ms. Kirk told us that Ms. Gardner entered the Health Clinic at approximately 11:10 A.M. and lit a cigarette in the waiting area. (7) At 11:20 A.M., Dr. Paul Stone examined Ms. Kirk. (8) Ms. Kirk explained to Ms. Gardner that smoking was not allowed in the Health Clinic and showed her the NO SMOKING signs posted on the walls. (9) Ms. Gardner ignored Ms. Kirk, and then grew very abusive and attacked her when Ms. Kirk insisted that she stop smoking. (10) Two witnesses, patients Edna Manning of 8937 4th Ave., Bronx, NY, and John Schultz of 357 149th Street, Bronx, NY, gave the same account of the incident as Ms. Kirk. (11) At 11:30 A.M., I read the prisoner her rights and placed her under arrest for violation of Penal Law Section 120.00 -Assault 3rd Degree. (12) At 11:35 A.M., I notified the 86th Precinct of Ms. Gardner's arrest and arranged for the transportation of the prisoner to the precinct. (13) At 11:40 A.M., Officer Colon escorted Ms. Gardner from the Nutrition Clinic to the patrolroom. (14) At 11:55 A.M., Police Officers Cranford, Shield #658, and Wargo, Shield #313, arrived at the facility to transport the prisoner to the precinct. (15) Officer Gray, Shield #936, assumed my post while I reported to the patrolroom to complete the necessary forms concerning the arrest.

6. At what time did Sergeant Lewis inform Officer John Clark of the disturbance in the Nutri-   6._____
tion Clinic?
_____ A.M.

    A. 11:00   B. 11:15   C. 11:16   D. 11:20

7. According to the Arrest Report and the Incident Report, how many witnesses gave the   7._____
same account of the incident as Ms. Kirk?

    A. 1   B. 2   C. 3   D. 4

8. What information on the Arrest Report is NOT included in the Incident Report?   8._____

    A. Date of Occurrence
    B. Victim's address
    C. Section of the Penal Law violated
    D. Assault 3rd Degree

9. Which sentence in the Incident Report is out of order in terms of the sequence of events?   9._____

    A. 3   B. 6   C. 11   D. 12

10. According to the Incident Report, at 11:40 A.M. Ms. Gardner was   10._____

    A. escorted to the patrolroom
    B. transported to the 86th Precinct
    C. examined by Dr. Paul Stone
    D. giving an account of the incident to Special Officers Clark and Colon

11. According to the Incident Report, which one of the following officers relieved Officer   11._____
Clark?
Officer

    A. Colon   B. Cranford   C. Wargo   D. Gray

12. Which section of the Arrest Report contains information that does NOT agree with Sen-   12._____
tence 11 of the Incident Report?
Section

    A. 1   B. 7   C. 8   D. 9

Question 13.

DIRECTIONS: Question 13 is to be answered SOLELY on the basis of the following information.

A Security Officer must investigate any complaint or incident which occurs in the facility,
whether he considers it is major or minor. The Officer must also interview the person(s)
involved in the incident in order to complete the necessary forms and reports.

13. Ms. Peters, a clerical worker at the facility, complains to Officer Tynan that a pen set, which had been given to her as a gift, was missing from her desk. She tells Officer Tynan that she knows the pen set was on her desk the previous day because she was using it for her work. Officer Tynan informs Ms. Peters that there is nothing he can do since the pen set was personal property and not facility property.
In this situation, Officer Tynan's response to Ms. Peters is

    13.____

    A. *correct,* chiefly because the pen set should not have been left out on a desk where it could be stolen
    B. *incorrect,* chiefly because a complaint of a loss of theft should be investigated and recorded
    C. *correct,* chiefly because Special Officers are only required to investigate a loss or theft of facility property
    D. *incorrect,* chiefly because Ms. Peters' work required use of the pen set

Question 14.

DIRECTIONS: Question 14 is to be answered SOLELY on the basis of the following information.

    Assume that Security Officers are responsible for recording in a personal memobook all of their routine and non-routine activities and occurrences for each tour of duty. Before starting a tour of duty, a Security Officer must enter in his personal memobook the date, tour, and assigned post. An entry shall be made to record each absence from duty, such as a regular day off, sick leave, annual leave, or holiday. During each tour, a Security Officer shall enter a full and accurate record of duties performed, changes in post assignment, absences from post, and the reason for each absence, and all other patrol business.

14. Security Officer Ella Lewis is assigned to Gotham Center Facility, where she works Monday through Friday on a 9:00 A.M. to 5:00 P.M. tour. Officer Lewis' regular days off are Saturday and Sunday. Officer Lewis worked on Wednesday, November 25, 2012. She was absent on Thursday, November 26, 2012, for Thanksgiving Holiday, and on Friday, November 27, 2012, for annual leave.
According to the information given above, which of the following entries is the FIRST entry that Officer Lewis should record in her memobook when she returns to work on November 30, 2012?

    14.____

    A. Saturday, 11/28/12 and Sunday, 11/29/12 - Regular days off
    B. Friday, 11/27/12 - Sick Leave
    C. Monday, 11/30/12 - On duty
    D. Thursday, 11/26/12 - Thanksgiving Holiday

Questions 15-16.

DIRECTIONS: Questions 15 and 16 are to be answered SOLELY on the basis of the following entries recorded by Security Officer Angela Russo in her memobook.

Date: January 8, 2012
Tour: 8:00 A.M. to 4:00 P.M.
Weather: Sunny and clear

7:30	Reported to *B* Command for Roll Call. Assigned to Post #2, *C* Building Emergency Room Corridor by Sergeant Robert Floyd. Break: 9:30 A.M. Meal: 1:30 P.M. Radio: #701
7:40	Arrived at Post #2 and relieved Special Officer Johnson, Shield #593.
7:45	On patrol - Post #2.
8:00	Post #2 - All secure at this time; conditions normal.
8:30	Fire Alarm Box 5-3-1 rings on 3rd Floor South in *C* Building. Upon arrival, Office Worker Molly Lewis reported that a waste-paper basket was on fire. Used fire extinguisher to put out fire.
8:50	Condition corrected; Incident Report prepared and submitted to Sergeant Floyd in *B* Command.
8:55	Resumed patrol of Post #2.
9:30	Relieved for break by Officer Tucker.
9:50	Resumed patrol of Post #2.
10:10	Disorderly person reported by Clinic Director Lila Jones on Ward C-32; Officer Bailey and myself responded. Clinic Director Jones informed officers that visitor Bradley Manna, male white, 19 years of age, 2 Park Place, Brooklyn, NY, is drunk and has been shouting insults to Clinic staff.
10:30	Condition corrected; Visitor Bradley Manna escorted off premises. *B* Command notified of incident.
10:40	Resumed patrol of Post #2.
11:40	Post #2 - All secure at this time.
12:40	Post #2 - All secure at this time.

15. The name of the Clinic Director who reported a disorderly person is   15.____

    A. Molly Lewis   B. Bradley Manna
    C. Lila Jones   D. Robert Floyd

16. Which of the following sets of officers responded to the report of a disorderly person on   16.____
    Ward C-32?
    Officers

    A. Johnson and Bailey   B. Russo and Tucker
    C. Johnson and Tucker   D. Russo and Bailey

17. Security Officer Mace is completing an entry in her memo-book. The entry has the fol-   17.____
lowing five sentences:
  1. I observed the defendant removing a radio from a facility vehicle.
  2. I placed the defendant under arrest and escorted him to the patrolroom.
  3. I was patrolling the facility parking lot.
  4. I asked the defendant to show identification.
  5. I determined that the defendant was not authorized to remove the radio.
The MOST logical order for these sentences to be entered in Officer Mace's memobook is

   A. 1, 3, 2, 4, 5   B. 2, 5, 4, 1, 3
   C. 3, 1, 4, 5, 2   D. 4, 5, 2, 1, 3

18. Security Officer Riley is completing an entry in his memo-book. The entry has the follow-   18.____
ing five sentences:
  1. Anna Jones admitted that she stole Mary Green's wallet.
  2. I approached the women and asked them who they were and why they were
     arguing.
  3. I arrested Anna Jones for stealing Mary Green's wallet.
  4. They identified themselves and Mary Green accused Anna Jones of stealing her
     wallet.
  5. I was in the lobby area when I observed two women arguing about a wallet.
The MOST logical order for these sentences to be entered
in Officer Riley's memobook is

   A. 2, 4, 1, 3, 5   B. 3, 1, 4, 5, 2
   C. 4, 1, 5, 2, 3   D. 5, 2, 4, 1, 3

19. Assume that Security Officer John Ryan is completing an entry in his memobook. The   19.____
entry has the following five sentences:
  1. I then cleared the immediate area of visitors and staff.
  2. I noticed smoke coming from a broom closet outside Room A71.
  3. Sergeant Mueller arrived with other officers to assist in clearing the area.
  4. Upon investigation, I determined the smoke was due to burning material in the
     broom closet.
  5. I pulled the corridor fire alarm and notified Sergeant Mueller of the fire.
The MOST logical order for these sentences to be entered in Officer Ryan's memobook is

   A. 2, 3, 4, 5, 1   B. 2, 4, 5, 1, 3
   C. 4, 1, 2, 3, 5   D. 5, 3, 2, 1, 4

20. Security Officer Hernandez is completing an entry in his memobook. The entry has the   20.____
following five sentences:
  1. I asked him to leave the premises immediately.
  2. A visitor complained that there was a strange man loitering in Clinic B hallway.
  3. I went to investigate and saw a man dressed in rags sitting on the floor of the
     hallway.
  4. As he walked out, he started yelling that he had no place to go.
  5. I asked to see identification, but he said that he did not have any.
The MOST logical order for these sentences to be entered in Officer Hernandez's
memobook is

A.	2, 3, 5, 1, 4	B.	3, 1, 2, 4, 5
C.	4, 1, 5, 2, 3	D.	3, 1, 5, 2, 4

21. Officer Hogan is completing an entry in his memobook. The entry has the following five   21.____
    sentences:
    1. When the fighting had stopped, I transmitted a message requesting medical
        assistance for Mr. Perkins.
    2. Special Officer Manning assisted me in stopping the fight.
    3. When I arrived at the scene, I saw a client, Adam Finley strike a facility
        employee, Peter Perkins.
    4. As I attempted to break up the fight, Special Officer Manning came on the scene.
    5. I received a radio message from Sergeant Valez to investigate a possible fight in
        progress in the waiting room.
    The MOST logical order for these sentences to be entered in Officer Hogan's memo-
    book is

A.	2, 1, 4, 5, 3	B.	3, 5, 2, 4,1
C.	4, 5, 3, 1, 2	D.	5, 3, 4, 2, 1

Questions 22-23.

DIRECTIONS: Questions 22 and 23 are to be answered SOLELY on the basis of the following
              information.

Assume that Security Officers may be assigned to the facility patrolroom and must follow
the guidelines below in documenting all routine and non-routine activities and occurrences in
the facility logbook.

At the beginning of each tour of duty, the Security Officer responsible for entering information in the logbook must transfer from the Roll Call Sheet to the logbook a list of all security
staff personnel assigned to that tour. This list is to be entered in order of the rank of the security staff member. All other entries in the facility logbook shall be recorded in chronological
order, in blue or black ink, and be neat and legible.

22. When recording the list of security staff personnel assigned to a tour, that entry shall be   22.____
    made in

    A. chronological order
    B. order of rank of security staff
    C. alphabetical order
    D. order of arrival at facility

23. A Security Officer has transmitted notification to the patrolroom that he has just issued a   23.____
    summons. The Security Officer responsible for documenting occurrences in the patrol-
    room logbook should record the information

    A. in red ink, immediately following the previous entry
    B. on a new page under the heading *Summonses Reported*
    C. in blue or black ink immediately following the previous entry
    D. on the last page of the logbook where it can be easily found

Question 24.

DIRECTIONS: Question 24 is to be answered SOLELY on the basis of the following information.

Assume that whenever a Security Officer is to begin a leave of absence, long-term sick leave, or other type of leave having an anticipated length of ten days or more, the officer shall surrender his or her security shield to his supervisor, who shall immediately forward it to Security Headquarters.

24.   Two male clients were fighting in the waiting room of North End Hospital. Officer Gary   24._____
Klott attempted to separate them and became involved in the altercation. Officer Klott sustained an injury to the right eye and was examined by a physician. The physician directed Officer Klott to stay home for a recovery period of 12 days. In this situation, Officer Klott should

   A.   surrender his shield to his supervisor
   B.   safeguard his shield in a safe place at home while he is recovering
   C.   surrender his shield to the physician
   D.   safeguard his shield with his uniform in his locker at the facility while he is recover-
ing

Question 25.

DIRECTIONS: Question 25 is to be answered SOLELY on the basis of the following information.

Assume that Security Officers are required to follow certain procedures when on post at a restricted area of a facility. They must inspect the identification of employees and passes of visitors, as well as all bags and packages carried by individuals who wish to enter the restricted area.

25.   Security Officer Stevens is assigned to a post at the Intensive Care Unit of Park View   25._____
Hospital, a restricted area. Officer Stevens is responsible for inspecting identification and passes, as well as all bags and packages carried by individuals who want to enter the Unit. He sees Mr. Craig approach. He knows Mr. Craig's wife is a patient in the Unit. Officer Stevens has seen Mr. Craig visit his wife every day for the past four days. Mr. Craig brings a small duffel bag filled with magazines each time he comes. Today, Officer Stevens checks Mr. Craig's visitor's pass but lets Mr. Craig enter the Unit without check-ing his duffel bag. In this situation, Officer Stevens' action is

   A.   *correct,* chiefly because he has checked to see that Mr. Craig has a visitor's pass
   B.   *incorrect,* chiefly because all packages and bags must be inspected before anyone
is allowed to enter a restricted area
   C.   *correct,* chiefly because he is familiar with Mr. Craig and knows that he only carries
magazines in his duffel bag
   D.   *incorrect,* chiefly because Mr. Craig should not be allowed to carry a bag or package into a restricted area of the facility

Question 26.

DIRECTIONS: Question 26 is to be answered SOLELY on the basis of the following information.

Assume that Special Officers must safeguard evidence in cases involving firearms. Special Officers must mark recovered bullets for identification purposes. The Officer who recovers the bullet must mark his or her initials and the date of recovery of the bullet on the base or on the nose of the bullet.

26.   On January 18, 2012, at 11:30 P.M., an unidentified person fired a shot at an unoccupied   26.___
security patrol car in the facility parking lot. Officer Debra Johnson was assigned to
investigate the matter. A fired bullet was recovered inside the patrol car by Officer
Johnson at 1:00 A.M. on January 19, 2012.
Officer Johnson should mark *D.J. 1/19/12* on

   A.   the base or the nose of the recovered bullet
   B.   the side of the recovered bullet
   C.   an envelope and place the recovered bullet inside
   D.   the side of the patrol car from which the bullet was recovered

Question 27.

DIRECTIONS: Question 27 is to be answered SOLELY on the basis of the following information.

Patrolroom Observers are officers who are assigned to observe events when individuals, other than security staff, are present in the patrolroom. According to facility guidelines, a Patrolroom Observer must be called to the patrolroom to serve as a witness whenever any individual is brought to the patrolroom for any reason by a Special Officer.

27.   Janet Childs, a client at Gotham Health Facility, was robbed in the facility's parking lot.   27.___
Ms. Childs was not harmed as a result of the incident, but she was upset. Special Officer
Grey escorted her to the patrol-room, where she remained until she felt better. While she
was waiting in the patrolroom, Officer Grey did not call a Patrolman Observer to the
patrolroom during the time that Ms. Childs was there.
In this situation, Officer Grey

   A.   should not have taken Ms. Childs to the patrolroom without special authorization
from his supervisor
   B.   was not required to call a Patrolroom Observer to the patrolroom since Ms. Childs
had not been placed under arrest
   C.   should have called a Patrolroom Observer to be present while Ms. Childs was in
the patrolroom
   D.   should have escorted Ms. Childs to the patrolroom and left her in the care of the
Special Officer assigned to the patrolroom

Question 28.

DIRECTIONS: Question 28 is to be answered SOLELY on the basis of the following information.

Special Officers escort individuals categorized as Emotionally Disturbed Persons to the hospital for observation or treatment when directed to do so. These individuals are transported to the hospital by Emergency Medical Service (EMS) ambulance. There must be one Special Officer present in the ambulance for each Emotionally Disturbed Person transferred to the hospital, along with an EMS Technician and the ambulance driver.

28.   Special Officers Patrick Lawson and Grace Martin have been assigned to escort two individuals categorized as Emotionally Disturbed Persons from that facility to a nearby hospital. The EMS ambulance, with an EMS Technician and ambulance driver, has arrived at the facility to transport the individuals. Officer Lawson then suggests to Officer Martin that it is not necessary for him to go to the hospital since the EMS Technician will be with Officer Martin in the ambulance.
In this situation, Officer Lawson's suggestion is

28.____

    A.   *correct,* since an EMS Technician will be present in the ambulance to accompany Officer Martin and the Emotionally Disturbed Persons to the hospital
    B.   *incorrect,* since one Special Officer must be present in the ambulance for each Emotionally Disturbed Person transported to the hospital
    C.   *correct,* since the Emotionally Disturbed Persons are unlikely to cause any disturbance inside the ambulance
    D.   *incorrect,* since two EMS Technicians must be present in the ambulance when only one Special Officer is escorting two Emotionally Disturbed Persons to the hospital

Questions 29-32.

DIRECTIONS: Questions 29 through 32 are to be answered on the basis of the following information.

Assume that information concerning new or updated policies and procedures are sometimes provided to facility security staff in the form of a memorandum from Security Headquarters.

Question 29.

DIRECTIONS: Question 29 is to be answered SOLELY on the basis of the following memorandum.

TO: All Security Officers
FROM: Security Headquarters
SUBJECT: Smoking Regulations

At times, Security Officers have been observed smoking while on duty at their assigned posts. This is strictly prohibited. If Officers feel that they must smoke, they may smoke during breaks or lunch period in designated areas. Officers may not smoke while on official duty. If any Officer is observed smoking while on post or while performing official duties, appropriate disciplinary action will be taken.

29. According to the above memorandum, Security Officers may   29.____

    A. smoke while on duty, as long as they are out of view of the public
    B. not smoke while on duty except when assigned to a post in a designated smoking area
    C. smoke on breaks or during lunch period in designated areas
    D. not smoke at any time when dressed in official uniform

Question 30.

DIRECTIONS: Question 30 is to be answered SOLELY on the basis of the following memo-randum.

TO: All Special Officers
FROM: Security Headquarters
SUBJECT: Safeguarding Shields and Identification Cards

Special Officers must ensure that their shields and identification cards are secure at all times. Should an officer become aware of the loss or theft of his shield or identification card, he shall immediately report such loss or theft to Security Headquarters.

30. According to the above memorandum, a Special Officer must   30.____

    A. report the loss or theft of his identification card to the nearest police precinct
    B. secure his shield in his locker at all times
    C. report the loss or theft of his shield or identification card to Security Headquarters immediately
    D. secure his identification card at Security Headquarters each night before leaving the facility

Question 31.

DIRECTIONS: Question 31 is to be answered SOLELY on the basis of the following memo-randum.

TO: All Security Officers
FROM: Security Headquarters
SUBJECT: Fire in the Facility

Special Officers must report immediately to assist at the scene of a fire when directed to do so by a supervisor. Officers shall remain at the scene and ensure that only authorized per-sonnel are in an area restricted by a fire emergency. Visitors and clients shall be directed to the nearest safe stairwell and out of the facility. Visitors and clients are not to use elevators to evacuate the area.

31. According to the above memorandum, a Security Officer should   31.____

    A. direct visitors and clients to the nearest elevator in case of fire
    B. report unauthorized personnel at a fire scene to the Fire Department
    C. escort visitors and clients down the nearest stairwell and out of the facility
    D. ensure that only authorized personnel are in an area restricted by a fire emergency

Question 32.

DIRECTIONS: Question 32 is to be answered SOLELY on the basis of the following memorandum.

TO: All Security Officers
FROM: Security Headquarters
SUBJECT: Reporting Unsafe Conditions

Security Officers shall report to their supervisors and appropriate facility staff any condition that could affect the safety or security of the facility. Conditions such as broken windows,
unlocked doors and water leaks should be reported.

32. According to the above memorandum, a Security Officer shall   32._____

    A. make recommendations to his superiors concerning other facility staff members
    B. correct all unsafe conditions such as broken windows
    C. report a condition such as a water leak to his supervisor and appropriate facility
        staff
    D. make recommendations to facility staff concerning doors to be left unlocked

33. Following are two sentences that may or may not be written in correct English: 33._____
    I. Special Officer Cleveland was attempting to calm an emotionally disturbed
       visitor.
    II. The visitor did not stops crying and calling for his wife.
Which one of the following statements is CORRECT?

    A. Only Sentence I is written in correct English.
    B. Only Sentence II is written in correct English.
    C. Sentences I and II are both written in correct English.
    D. Neither Sentence I nor Sentence II is written in correct English.

34. Following are two sentences that may or may not be written in correct English: 34._____
    I. While on patrol, I observes a vagrant loitering near the drug dispensary.
    II. I escorted the vagrant out of the building and off the premises.
Which one of the following statements is CORRECT?

    A. Only Sentence I is written in correct English.
    B. Only Sentence II is written in correct English.
    C. Sentences I and II are both written in correct English.
    D. Neither Sentence I nor Sentence II is written in correct English.

35. Following are two sentences that may or may not be written in correct English: 35._____
    I. At 4:00 P.M., Sergeant Raymond told me to evacuate the waiting area imme-
      diately due to a bomb threat.
    II. Some of the clients did not want to leave the building.
Which one of the following statements is CORRECT?

    A. Only Sentence I is written in correct English.
    B. Only Sentence II is written in correct English.
    C. Sentences I and II are both written in correct English.
    D. Neither Sentence I nor Sentence II is written in correct English.

KEY (CORRECT ANSWERS)

1.	C		16.	D
2.	B		17.	C
3.	A		18.	D
4.	D		19.	B
5.	A		20.	A
6.	B		21.	D
7.	B		22.	B
8.	B		23.	C
9.	B		24.	A
10.	A		25.	B
11.	D		26.	A
12.	C		27.	C
13.	B		28.	B
14.	D		29.	C
15.	C		30.	C

31.	D
32.	C
33.	A
34.	B
35.	C

———

EXAMINATION SECTION
TEST 1

Questions 1-4.

Questions 1 to 4 measure your ability to recognize objects, people, events, parts of maps, or crime, accident, or other scenes to which you have been exposed.

Below and on the following pages are twenty illustrations. Study them carefully. In the test, you will be shown pairs of drawings. For each pair, you will be asked which is or are from the twenty illustrations in this part.

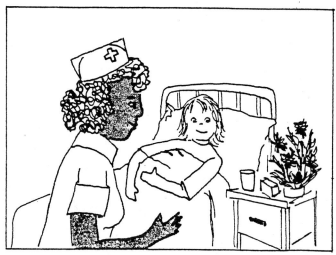

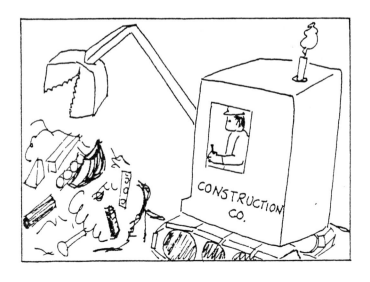

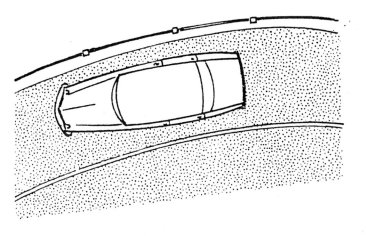

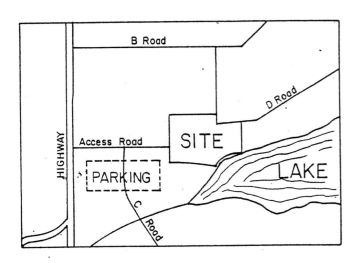

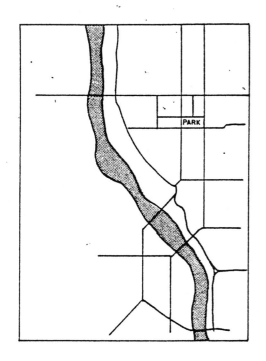

Questions 1-4.

DIRECTIONS: In Questions 1 to 4, select the choice that corresponds to the scene(s) that is(are) from the illustrations for this section. *PRINT THE LETTER OF THE CORRECT ANSWER IN THE SPACE AT THE RIGHT.*

1.

1._____

I

II.

A. I *only*
C. Both I and II

B. II *only*
D. Neither I nor II

2.

2._____

I.

II.

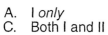

A. I *only*
C. Both I and II

B. II *only*
D. Neither I nor II

3.   I.   II.   3._____

A. I only
C. Both I and II

B. II only
D. Neither I nor II

4.   I.   II.   4._____

A. I only
C. Both I and II

B. II only
D. Neither I nor II

Questions 5-6.

DIRECTIONS: Questions 5 and 6 measure your ability to notice and interpret details accurately. You will be shown a picture, below, and then asked a set of questions about the picture. You do NOT need to memorize this picture. You may look at the picture when answering the questions.

5. Details in the picture lend some support to or do NOT tend to contradict which of the fol- 5.____
   lowing statements about the person who occupies the room?
   I.   The person is very careless.
   II. The person smokes
   The CORRECT answer is:

   A. I *only*   B. II *only*
   C. Both I and II   D. Neither I nor II

6. The number on the piece of paper on the desk is *most likely* a   6.____

   A. ZIP code   B. street number
   C. social security number   D. telephone area code

Questions 7-10.

DIRECTIONS: Questions 7 to 10 measure your ability to recognize objects or people in differ-
              ing views, contexts, or situations. Each question consists of three pictures; one
              labeled *I,* and one labeled *II.* In each question, you are to determine whether *A
              - I only, B - II only, C - Both I and II,* or *D - Neither I nor II* COULD be the Sub-
              ject.
              The Subject is *always* ONE person or ONE object. The Subject-picture shows
              the object or person as it, he, or she appeared at the time of initial contact. Pic-
              tures I and II show objects from a different viewpoint than that of the Subject-
              picture. For example, if the Subject-picture presents a front view, I and II may
              present back views, side views, or a back and a side view. Also, art objects may
              be displayed differently, may have a different base or frame or method of hang-
              ing.

When the Subject is a person, I or II will be a picture of a different person or will be a picture of the same person after some change has taken place: The person may have made a deliberate attempt to alter his or her appearance, such as wearing (or taking off) a wig, growing (or shaving off) a beard or mustache, or dressing as a member of the opposite sex. The change may also be a natural one, such as changing a hair style, changing from work clothes to play clothes or from play clothes to work clothes, or growing older, thinner, or fatter. *None has had cosmetic surgery.*

7.   7._____

Subject   **I.**   **II.**

A. I *only*   B. II *only*
C. Both I and II   D. Neither I nor II

8.   8._____

Subject   **I.**   **II.**

A. I *only*   B. II *only*
C. Both I and II   D. Neither I nor II

9.

Subject   **I.**   **II.**

 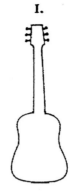

A. I *only*   B. II *only*
C. Both I and II   D. Neither I nor II

10.

Subject   **I.**   **II.**

A. I *only*   B. II *only*
C. Both I and II   D. Neither I nor II

_____

KEY (CORRECT ANSWERS)

1.	B	6.	B
2.	D	7.	D
3.	A	8.	A
4.	A	9.	D
5.	B	10.	D

_____

EVALUATING INFORMATION AND EVIDENCE
EXAMINATION SECTION
TEST 1

DIRECTIONS: Each question or incomplete statement is followed by several suggested answers or completions. Select the one that BEST answers the question or completes the statement. *PRINT THE LETTER OF THE CORRECT ANSWER IN THE SPACE AT THE RIGHT.*

Questions 1 -9

Questions 1 through 9 measure your ability to (1) determine whether statements from witnesses say essentially the same thing and (2) determine the evidence needed to make it reasonably certain that a particular conclusion is true.

1. Which of the following pairs of statements say essentially the same thing in two different ways?   1.____

   I. If you get your feet wet, you will catch a cold.
       If you catch a cold, you must have gotten your feet wet.
   II. If I am nominated, I will run for office.
       I will run for office only if I am nominated.

   A. I only
   B. I and II
   C. II only
   D. Neither I nor II

2. Which of the following pairs of statements say essentially the same thing in two different ways?   2.____

   I. The enzyme Rhopsin cannot be present if the bacterium Trilox is absent.
       Rhopsin and Trilox always appear together.
   II. A member of PENSA has an IQ of at least 175.
       A person with an IQ of less than 175 is not a member of PENSA.

   A. I only
   B. I and II
   C. II only
   D. Neither I nor II

3. Which of the following pairs of statements say essentially the same thing in two different ways?   3.____

   I. None of Finer High School's sophomores will be going to the prom.
       No student at Finer High School who is going to the prom is a sophomore.
   II. If you have 20/20 vision, you may carry a firearm.
       You may not carry a firearm unless you have 20/20 vision.

   A. I only
   B. I and II
   C. II only
   D. Neither I nor II

4. Which of the following pairs of statements say essentially the same thing in two different 4.____
   ways?

       I.   If the family doesn't pay the ransom, they will never see their son again.
           It is necessary for the family to pay the ransom in order for them to see
           their son again.
       II. If it is raining, I am carrying an umbrella.
           If I am carrying an umbrella, it is raining.

       A. I only
       B. I and II
       C. II only
       D. Neither I nor II

5. Summary of Evidence Collected to Date: 5.____
   In the county's maternity wards, over the past year, only one baby was born who did
   not share a birthday with any other baby.
   Prematurely Drawn Conclusion: At least one baby was born on the same day as
   another baby in the county's maternity wards.
   Which of the following pieces of evidence, if any, would make it *reasonably certain* that
   the conclusion drawn is true?

       A. More than 365 babies were born in the county's maternity wards over the past year
       B. No pairs of twins were born over the past year in the county's maternity wards
       C. More than one baby was born in the county's maternity wards over the past year
       D. None of these

6. Summary of Evidence Collected to Date: 6.____
   Every claims adjustor for MetroLife drives only a Ford sedan when on the job.
   Prematurely Drawn Conclusion: A person who works for MetroLife and drives a Ford
   sedan is a claims adjustor.
   Which of the following pieces of evidence, if any, would make it *reasonably certain* that
   the conclusion drawn is true?

       A. Most people who work for MetroLife are claims adjustors
       B. Some people who work for MetroLife are not claims adjustors
       C. Most people who work for MetroLife drive Ford sedans
       D. None of these

7. Summary of Evidence Collected to Date: 7.____
   Mason will speak to Zisk if Zisk will speak to Ronaldson.
   Prematurely Drawn Conclusion: Jones will not speak to Zisk if Zisk will speak to
   Ronaldson
   Which of the following pieces of evidence, if any, would make it *reasonably certain* that
   the conclusion drawn is true?

       A. If Zisk will speak to Mason, then Ronaldson will not speak to Jones
       B. If Mason will speak to Zisk, then Jones will not speak to Zisk
       C. If Ronaldson will speak to Jones, then Jones will speak to Ronaldson
       D. None of these

8. <u>Summary of Evidence Collected to Date:</u> 8.____
   No blue lights on the machine are indicators for the belt drive status.
   <u>Prematurely Drawn Conclusion:</u> Some of the lights on the lower panel are not indicators for the belt drive status.
   Which of the following pieces of evidence, if any, would make it *reasonably certain* that the conclusion drawn is true?

   A. No lights on the machine's lower panel are blue
   B. An indicator light for the machine's belt drive status is either green or red
   C. Some lights on the machine's lower panel are blue
   D. None of these

9. <u>Summary of Evidence Collected to Date:</u> 9.____
   Of the four Sweeney sisters, two are married, three have brown eyes, and three are doctors.
   <u>Prematurely Drawn Conclusion:</u> Two of the Sweeney sisters are brown-eyed, married doctors.
   Which of the following pieces of evidence, if any, would make it *reasonably certain* that the conclusion drawn is true?

   A. The sister who does not have brown eyes is married
   B. The sister who does not have brown eyes is not a doctor, and one who is not married is not a doctor
   C. Every Sweeney sister with brown eyes is a doctor
   D. None of these

Questions 10-14

Questions 10 through 14 refer to Map #5 and measure your ability to orient yourself within a given section of town, neighborhood or particular area. Each of the questions describes a starting point and a destination. Assume that you are driving a car in the area shown on the map accompanying the questions. Use the map as a basis for the shortest way to get from one point to another without breaking the law.

On the map, a street marked by arrows, or by arrows and the words "One Way," indicates one-way travel, and should be assumed to be one-way for the entire length, even when there are breaks or jogs in the street. EXCEPTION: A street that does not have the same name over the full length.

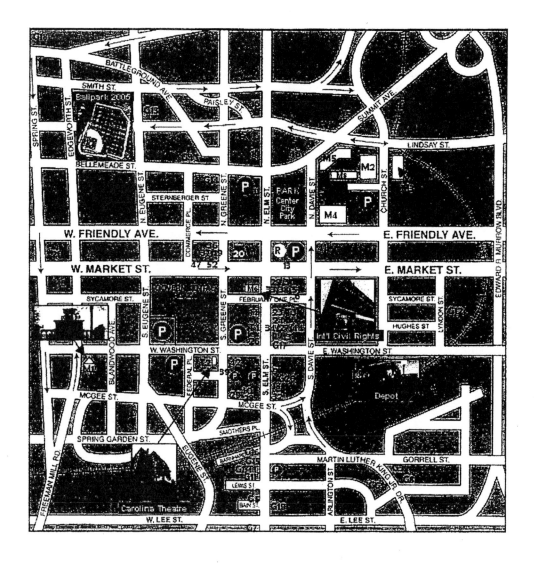

Map #5

10. The shortest legal way from the depot to Center City Park is

    A. north on Church, west on Market, north on Elm
    B. east on Washington, north on Edward R. Murrow Blvd., west on Friendly Ave.
    C. west on Washington, north on Greene, east on Market, north on Davie
    D. north on Church, west on Friendly Ave.

10.____

11. The shortest legal way from the Governmental Plaza to the ballpark is

    A. west on Market, north on Edgeworth
    B. west on Market, north on Eugene
    C. north on Greene, west on Lindsay
    D. north on Commerce Place, west on Bellemeade

11.____

12. The shortest legal way from the International Civil Rights Building to the building marked "M3" on the map is   12._____

    A. east on February One Place, north on Davie, east on Friendly Ave., north on Church
    B. south on Elm, west on Washington, north on Greene, east on Market, north on Church
    C. north on Elm, east on Market, north on Church
    D. north on Elm, east on Lindsay, south on Church

13. The shortest legal way from the ballpark to the Carolina Theatre is   13._____

    A. east on Lindsay, south on Greene
    B. south on Edgeworth, east on Friendly Ave., south on Greene
    C. east on Bellemeade, south on Elm, west on Washington
    D. south on Eugene, east on Washington

14. A car traveling north or south on Church Street may NOT go   14._____

    A. west onto Friendly Ave.
    B. west onto Lindsay
    C. east onto Market
    D. west onto Smith

Questions 15-19

Questions 15 through 19 refer to Figure #5, on the following page, and measure your ability to understand written descriptions of events. Each question presents a description of an accident or event and asks you which of the five drawings in Figure #5 BEST represents it.

In the drawings, the following symbols are used:

Moving vehicle: ⬆   Non-moving vehicle: ⬆

Pedestrian or bicyclist: ●

The path and direction of travel of a vehicle or pedestrian is indicated by a solid line.

The path and direction of travel of each vehicle or pedestrian directly involved in a collision from the point of impact is indicated by a dotted line.

In the space at the right, print the letter of the drawing that best fits the descriptions written below:

15. A driver heading south on Ohio runs a red light and strikes the front of a car headed west on Grand. He glances off and leaves the roadway at the southwest corner of Grand and Ohio.   15._____

16. A driver heading east on Grand drifts into the oncoming lane as it travels through the intersection of Grand and Ohio, and strikes an oncoming car head-on.   16._____

17. A driver heading east on Grand veers into the oncoming lane, sideswipes a westbound car and overcorrects as he swerves back into his lane. He leaves the roadway near the southeast corner of Grand and Ohio.

17.____

18. A driver heading east on Grand strikes the front of a car that is traveling north on Ohio and has run a red light. After striking the front of the northbound car, the driver veers left and leaves the roadway at the northeast corner of Grand and Ohio.

18.____

19. A driver heading east on Grand is traveling above the speed limit and clips the rear end of another eastbound car. The driver then veers to the left and leaves the roadway at the northeast corner of Grand and Ohio.

19.____

FIGURE #5

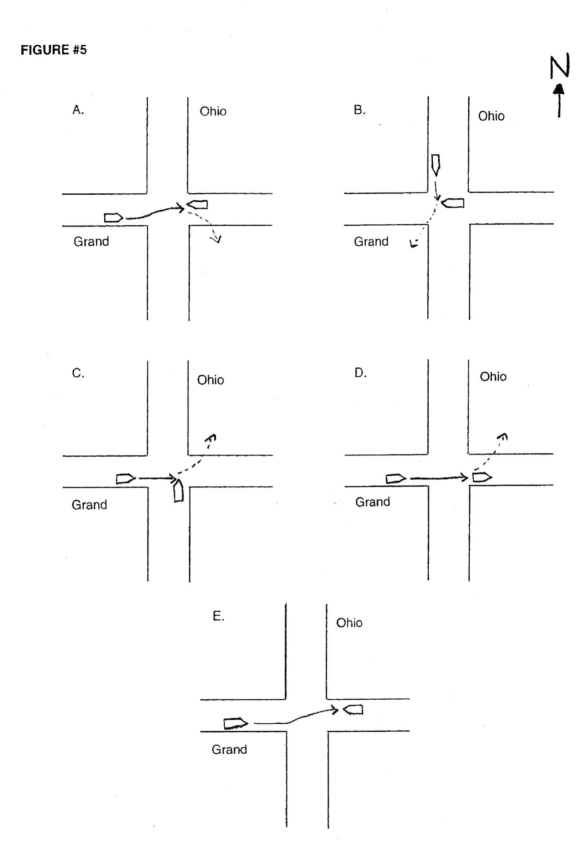

Questions 20-22

In questions 20 through 22, choose the word or phrase CLOSEST in meaning to the word or phrase printed in capital letters.

20. PETITION

    A. appeal
    B. law
    C. oath
    D. opposition

20.____

21. MALPRACTICE

    A. commission
    B. mayhem
    C. error
    D. misconduct

21.____

22. EXONERATE

    A. incriminate
    B. accuse
    C. lengthen
    D. acquit

22.____

Questions 23-25

Questions 23 through 25 measure your ability to do fieldwork-related arithmetic. Each question presents a separate arithmetic problem for you to solve.

23. Officers Lane and Bryant visited another city as part of an investigation. Because each is from a different precinct, they agree to split all expenses. With her credit card, Lane paid $70 for food and $150 for lodging. Bryant wrote checks for gas ($50) and entertainment ($40).
    How much does Bryant owe Lane?

23.____

    A. $65   B. $90   C. $155   D. $210

24. In a remote mountain pass, two search-and-rescue teams, one from Silverton and one from Durango, combine to look for a family that disappeared in a recent snowstorm. The combined team is composed of 20 members. Which of the following statements could NOT be true?

24.____

    A. The Durango team has a dozen members
    B. The Silverton team has only one member
    C. The Durango team has two more members than the Silverton team
    D. The Silverton team has one more member than the Durango team

25. Three people in the department share a vehicle for a period of one year. The average number of miles traveled per month by each person is 150. How many miles will be added to the car's odometer at the end of the year?

25.____

    A. 1,800   B. 2,400   C. 3,600   D. 5,400

KEY (CORRECT ANSWERS)

1.	D	11.	D
2.	C	12.	C
3.	A	13.	D
4.	A	14.	D
5.	A	15.	B
6.	D	16.	E
7.	B	17.	A
8.	C	18.	C
9.	B	19.	D
10.	D	20.	A

21.	D
22.	D
23.	A
24.	D
25.	D

SOLUTIONS TO QUESTIONS 1-9

P implies Q = original statement

Not Q implies not P = contrapositive of the original statement. A statement and its contrapositive are logically equivalent.

Q implies P = converse of the original statement.

Not P implies not Q = inverse of the original statement. The converse and inverse of an original statement are logically equivalent.

P implies Q = Not P or Q.

#1. The correct answer is **D**. In items I and II, each statement is the converses of the other. A converse of a statement is not equivalent to its original statement.

#2. The correct answer is **C**. In item I, the first statement is equivalent to "If Trilox is absent, then Rhopsin is also absent." But this does <u>not</u> imply that if Trilox is present, so too must Rhopsin be present. In item II, each statement is the contrapositive of the other. Thus, they are equivalent.

#3. The correct answer is **A**. In item I, the first statement tells us that if a student is a sophomore, he/she will not go to the prom. The second statement is equivalent to "If a student does attend the prom, he/she is not a sophomore." This is the contrapositive of the first statement, (so it is equivalent to it).

#4. The correct answer is **A**. In item I, the second statement can be written as "If the family sees their son again, then they must have paid the ransom." This is the contrapositive of the first statement. In item II, these statements are converses of each other; thus, they are not equivalent.

#5. The correct answer is **A**. If more than 365 babies were born in the county in one year, then at least two babies must share the same birthday.

#6. The correct answer is **A**. Given that most people who work for MetroLife are claims adjustors, plus the fact that all claims adjustors drive only a Ford sedan, it is a reasonable conclusion that any person who drives a Ford sedan and works for MetroLife is a claims adjustor.

#7. The correct answer is **B**. Jones will not speak to Zisk if Zisk will speak to Ronaldson, which <u>will</u> happen if Mason will speak to Zisk.

#8. The correct answer is **C**. We are given that blue lights are never an indicator for the drive belt status. If some of the lights on the lower panel of the machine are blue, then it is reasonable to conclude that some of the lights on the lower panel are not indicators for the drive belt status.

#9. The correct answer is **D**. It is possible to have the following situation: Sister 1 is not married, does not have brown eyes, and is a doctor; each of sisters 2 and 3 is married, has brown eyes and is a doctor; sister 4 is not married, has brown eyes, and is not a doctor. None of choices A, B, or C would lead to the situation as described above.

TEST 2

DIRECTIONS: Each question or incomplete statement is followed by several suggested answers or completions. Select the one that BEST answers the question or completes the statement. *PRINT THE LETTER OF THE CORRECT ANSWER IN THE SPACE AT THE RIGHT.*

Questions 1-9

Questions 1 through 9 measure your ability to (1) determine whether statements from witnesses say essentially the same thing and (2) determine the evidence needed to make it reasonably certain that a particular conclusion is true.
To do well on this part of the test, you do NOT have to have a working knowledge of police procedures and techniques. Nor do you have to have any more familiarity with criminals and criminal behavior than that acquired from reading newspapers, listening to radio or watching TV. To do well in this part, you must read and reason carefully.

1. Which of the following pairs of statements say essentially the same thing in two different   1._____
    ways?
    I.   If there is life on Mars, we should fund NASA.
         Either there is life on Mars, or we should not fund NASA.
    II. All Eagle Scouts are teenage boys.
         All teenage boys are Eagle Scouts.

    A.   I only
    B.   I and II
    C.   II only
    D.   Neither I nor II

2. Which of the following pairs of statements say essentially the same thing in two different   2._____
    ways?
    I.   If that notebook is missing its front cover, it definitely belongs to Carter.
         Carter's notebook is the only one missing its front cover.
    II. If it's hot, the pool is open.
         The pool is open if it's hot.

    A.   I only
    B.   I and II
    C.   II only
    D.   Neither I nor II

3. Which of the following pairs of statements say essentially the same thing in two different   3._____
    ways?
    I.   Nobody who works at the mill is without benefits.
         Everyone who works at the mill has benefits.
    II. We will fund the program only if at least 100 people sign the petition.
         Either we will fund the program or at least 100 people will sign the petition.

    A.   I only
    B.   I and II
    C.   II only
    D.   Neither I nor II

4. Which of the following pairs of statements say essentially the same thing in two different ways?   4.____

    I. If the new parts arrive, Mr. Luther's request has been answered.
    Mr. Luther requested new parts to arrive.
    II. The machine's test cycle will not run unless the operation cycle is not running.
    The machine's test cycle must be running in order for the operation cycle to run.

    A. I only
    B. I and II
    C. II only
    D. Neither I nor II

5. Summary of Evidence Collected to Date: 5.____

    I. To become a member of the East Side Crips, a kid must be either "jumped in" or steal a squad car without getting caught.
    II. Sid, a kid on the East Side, was caught stealing a squad car.

Prematurely Drawn Conclusion: Sid did not become a member of the East Side Crips.
Which of the following pieces of evidence, if any, would make it *reasonably certain* that the conclusion drawn is true?

    A. "Jumping in" is not allowed in prison
    B. Sid was not "jumped in"
    C. Sid's stealing the squad car had nothing to do with wanting to join the East Side Crips
    D. None of these

6. Summary of Evidence Collected to Date: 6.____

    I. Jones, a Precinct 8 officer, has more arrests than Smith.
    II. Smith and Watson have exactly the same number of arrests.

Prematurely Drawn Conclusion: Watson is not a Precinct 8 officer.
Which of the following pieces of evidence, if any, would make it *reasonably certain* that the conclusion drawn is true?

    A. All the officers in Precinct 8 have more arrests than Watson
    B. All the officers in Precinct 8 have fewer arrests than Watson
    C. Watson has fewer arrests than Jones
    D. None of these

7. Summary of Evidence Collected to Date: 7.____

    I. Twenty one-dollar bills are divided among Frances, Kerry and Brian.
    II. If Kerry gives her dollar bills to Frances, then Frances will have more money than Brian.

Prematurely Drawn Conclusion: Frances has twelve dollars.
Which of the following pieces of evidence, if any, would make it *reasonably certain* that the conclusion drawn is true?

    A. If Brian gives his dollars to Kerry, then Kerry will have more money than Frances
    B. Brian has two dollars
    C. If Kerry gives her dollars to Brian, Brian will still have less money than Frances
    D. None of these

8. <u>Summary of Evidence Collected to Date:</u>   8._____
       I.   The street sweepers will be here at noon today.
      II. Residents on the west side of the street should move their cars before noon.
<u>Prematurely Drawn Conclusion:</u> Today is Wednesday.
Which of the following pieces of evidence, if any, would make it *reasonably certain* that the conclusion drawn is true?

    A.   The street sweepers never sweep the east side of the street on Wednesday
    B.   The street sweepers arrive at noon every other day
    C.   There is no parking allowed on the west side of the street on Wednesday
    D.   None of these

9. <u>Summary of Evidence Collected to Date:</u>   9._____
The only time the warning light comes on is when there is a power surge.
<u>Prematurely Drawn Conclusion:</u> The warning light does not come on if the air conditioner is not running.
Which of the following pieces of evidence, if any, would make it *reasonably certain* that the conclusion drawn is true?

    A.   The air conditioner does not turn on if the warning light is on
    B.   Sometimes a power surge is caused by the dishwasher
    C.   There is only a power surge when the air conditioner turns on
    D.   None of these

Questions 10-14

Questions 10 through 14 refer to Map #6 and measure your ability to orient yourself within a given section of town, neighborhood or particular area. Each of the questions describes a starting point and a destination. Assume that you are driving a car in the area shown on the map accompanying the questions. Use the map as a basis for the shortest way to get from one point to another without breaking the law.

On the map, a street marked by arrows, or by arrows and the words "One Way," indicates one-way travel, and should be assumed to be one-way for the entire length, even when there are breaks or jogs in the street. EXCEPTION: A street that does not have the same name over the full length.

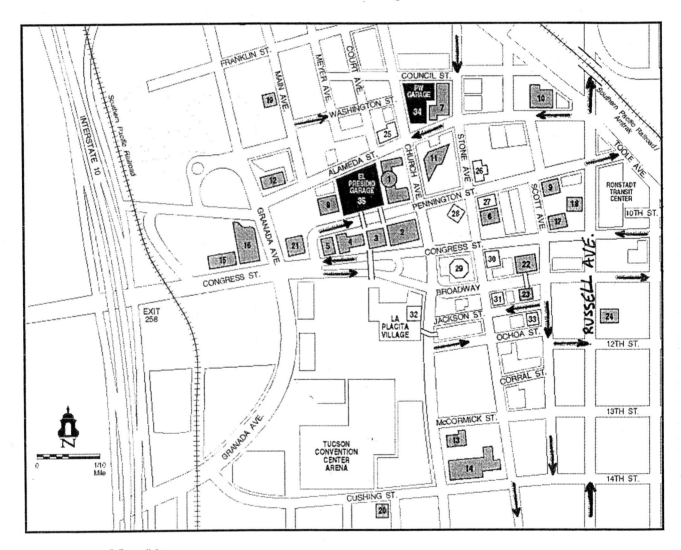

Map #6

PIMA COUNTY

1 Old Courthouse
2 Superior Court Building
3 Administration Building
4 Health and Welfare Building
5 Mechanical Building
6 Legal Services Building
7 County/City Public Works Center

CITY OF TUCSON

8 City Hall
9 City Hall Annex
10 Alameda Plaza City Court Building
11 Public Library - Main Branch
12 Tucson Water Building
13 Fire Department Headquarters
14 Police Department Building

10. The shortest legal way from the Public Library to the Alameda Plaza City Court Building   10.____
    is

    A. north on Stone Ave., east on Alameda
    B. south on Stone Ave., east on Congress, north on Russell Ave., west on Alameda
    C. south on Stone Ave., east on Pennington, north on Russell Ave., west on Alameda
    D. south on Church Ave., east on Pennington, north on Russell Ave., west on Alameda

11. The shortest legal way from City Hall to the Police Department is   11.____

    A. east on Congress, south on Scott Ave., west on 14th
    B. east on Pennington, south on Stone Ave.
    C. east on Congress, south on Stone Ave.
    D. east on Pennington, south on Church Ave.

12. The shortest legal way from the Tucson Water Building to the Legal Service Building is   12.____

    A. south on Granada Ave., east on Congress, north to east on Pennington, south on Stone Ave.
    B. east on Alameda, south on Church Ave., east on Pennington, south on Stone Ave.
    C. north on Granada Ave., east on Washington, south on Church Ave., east on Pennington, south on Stone Ave.
    D. south on Granada Ave., east on Cushing, north on Stone Ave.

13. The shortest legal way from the Tucson Convention Center Arena to the City Hall Annex   13.____
    is

    A. west on Cushing, north on Granada Ave., east on Congress, east on Broadway, north on Scott Ave.
    B. east on Cushing, north on Church Ave., east on Pennington
    C. east on Cushing, north on Russell Ave., west on Pennington
    D. east on Cushing, north on Stone Ave., east on Pennington

14. The shortest legal way from the Ronstadt Transit Center to the Fire Department is   14.____

    A. west on Pennington , south on Stone Ave., west on McCormick
    B. west on Congress, south on Russell Ave., west on 13th
    C. west on Congress, south on Church Ave.
    D. west on Pennington, south on Church Ave.

Questions 15-19

Questions 15 through 19 refer to Figure #6, on the following page, and measure your ability to understand written descriptions of events. Each question presents a description of an accident or event and asks you which of the five drawings in Figure #6 BEST represents it.

In the drawings, the following symbols are used:

Moving vehicle: ◊   Non-moving vehicle: ◆

Pedestrian or bicyclist: ●

The path and direction of travel of a vehicle or pedestrian is indicated by a solid line.

The path and direction of travel of each vehicle or pedestrian directly involved in a collision from the point of impact is indicated by a dotted line.

In the space at the right, print the letter of the drawing that best fits the descriptions written below:

15. A bicyclist heading southwest on Rose travels into the intersection, sideswipes a car that is heading east on Page, and veers right, leaving the roadway at the northwest corner of Page and Mill.

15.____

16. A driver traveling north on Mill swerves right to avoid a bicyclist that is traveling southwest on Rose. The driver strikes the rear end of a car parked on Rose. The bicyclist continues through the intersection and travels west on Page.

16.____

17. A bicyclist heading southwest on Rose travels into the intersection, sideswipes a car that is heading east on Page, and veers right, striking the rear end of a car parked in the westbound lane on Page.

17.____

18. A driver traveling east on Page swerves left to avoid a bicyclist that is traveling southwest on Rose. The driver strikes the rear end of a car parked on Mill. The bicyclist continues through the intersection and travels west on Page.

18.____

19. A bicyclist heading southwest on Rose enters the intersection and sideswipes a car that is swerving left to avoid her. The bicyclist veers left and collides with a car parked in the southbound lane on Mill. The driver of the car veers left and collides with a car parked in the northbound lane on Mill.

19.____

FIGURE #6

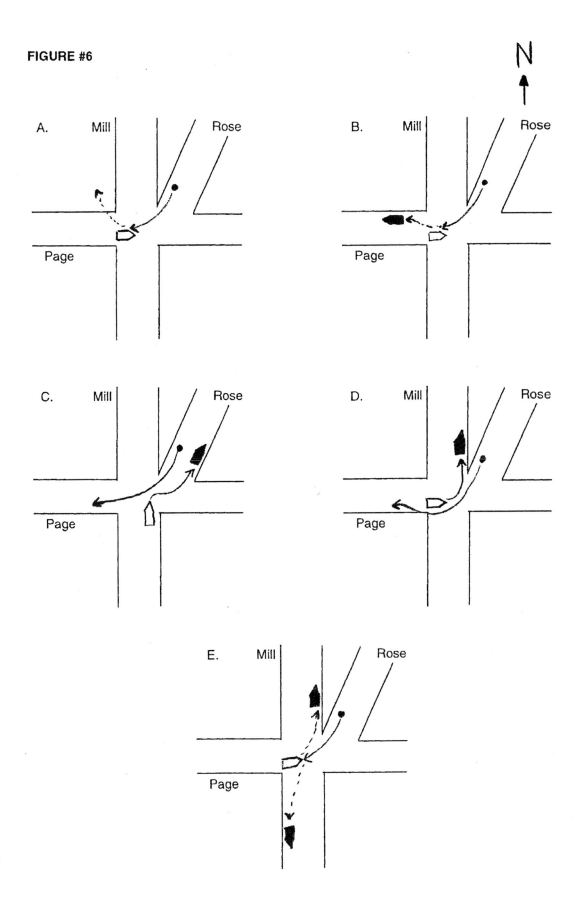

Questions 20-22

In questions 20 through 22, choose the word or phrase CLOSEST in meaning to the word or phrase printed in capital letters.

20. WAIVE

    A. cease
    B. surrender
    C. prevent
    D. die

20.____

21. DEPOSITION

    A. settlement
    B. deterioration
    C. testimony
    D. character

21.____

22. IMMUNITY

    A. exposure
    B. accusation
    C. protection
    D. exchange

22.____

Questions 23-25

Questions 23 through 25 measure your ability to do fieldwork-related arithmetic. Each question presents a separate arithmetic problem for you to solve.

23. Dean, a claims investigator, is reading a 445-page case record in his spare time at work. He has already read 157 pages. If Dean reads 24 pages a day, he should finish reading the rest of the record in _____ days.

    A. 7   B. 12   C. 19   D. 24

23.____

24. The Fire Department owns four cars. The Department of Sanitation owns twice as many cars as the Fire Department. The Department of Parks and Recreation owns one fewer car than the Department of Sanitation. The Department of Parks and Recreation is buying new tires for each of its cars. Each tire costs $100. How much is the Department of Parks and Recreation going to spend on tires?

    A. $400   B. $2,800   C. $3,200   D. $4,900

24.____

25. A dance hall is about 5,000 square feet. The local ordinance does not allow more than 50 people per every 100 square feet of commercial space. The maximum occupancy of the hall is

    A. 500   B. 2,500   C. 5,000   D. 25,000

25.____

KEY (CORRECT ANSWERS)

1.	D		11.	D
2.	B		12.	A
3.	A		13.	B
4.	A		14.	C
5.	B		15.	A
6.	D		16.	C
7.	D		17.	B
8.	D		18.	D
9.	C		19.	E
10.	C		20.	B

21.	C
22.	C
23.	B
24.	B
25.	B

———

SOLUTIONS TO QUESTIONS 1-9

P implies Q = original statement

Not Q implies not P = contrapositive of the original statement. A statement and its contrapositive are logically equivalent.

Q implies P = converse of the original statement.

Not P implies not Q = inverse of the original statement. The converse and inverse of an original statement are logically equivalent.

P implies Q = Not P or Q.

#1. The correct answer is **D**. For item I, the second statement should be "Either there is no life on Mars or we should fund NASA" in order to be logically equivalent to the first statement. For item II, the statements are converses of each other; thus they are not equivalent.

#2. The correct answer is **B**. In item I, this is an example of P implies Q and Q implies P. In this case, P = the notebook is missing its cover and Q = the notebook belongs to Carter. In item II, the ordering of the words is changed, but the If P then Q is exactly the same. P = it is hot and Q = the pool is open.

#3. The correct answer is **A**. For item I, if nobody is without benefits, then everybody has benefits. For item II, the second equivalent statement should be "either we will not fund the program or at least 100 people will sign the petition."

#4. The answer is **D**. For item I, the first statement is an implication, whereas the second statement mentions only one part of the implication (new parts are requested) and says nothing about the other part. For item II, the first statement is equivalent to "if the operating cycle is not running, then the test cycle will run." The second statement is equivalent to "if the operating cycle is running, then the test cycle will run." So, these statements in item II are not equivalent.

#5. The correct answer is **B**. Since Sid did not steal a car and avoid getting caught, the only other way he could become a Crips member would be "jumped in." Choice B tells us that Sid was not "jumped in," so we conclude that he did not become a member of the Crips.

#6. The correct answer is **D**. Since Smith and Watson have the same number of arrests, Watson must have fewer arrests than Jones. This means that each of choices A and B is impossible. Choice C would also not reveal whether or not Watson is a Precinct 8 officer.

#7. The correct answer is **D**. Exact dollar amounts still cannot be ascertained by using any of the other choices.

#8. The correct answer is **A**. The street sweepers never sweep on the east side of the street on Wednesday; however, they will be here at noon today. This implies that they will sweep on the west side of the street. Since the residents should move their cars before noon, we can conclude that today is Wednesday.

#9. The correct answer is **C**. We start with W implies P, where W = warning light comes on and P = power surge. Choice C would read as P implies A, where A = air conditioning is running. Combining these statements leads to W implies A. The conclusion can be read as: Not A implies Not W, which is equivalent to W implies A.

SCANNING MAPS

One section of the exam tests your ability to orient yourself within a given region on a map. Using the map accompanying questions 1 through 3, choose the best way of getting from one point to another.

The New Bridge is closed to traffic because it has a broken span.

MAP 1

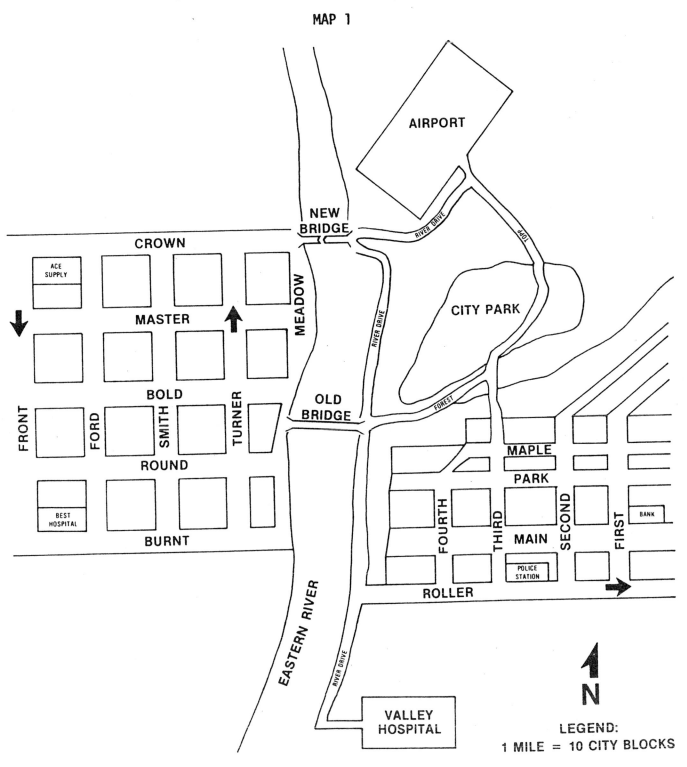

Arrows (———▶) indicate one-way traffic and direction of traffic. A street marked by an arrow is one way for the entire length of the street.

Sample Questions

1. Officers in a patrol car which is at the Airport receive a call for assistance at Best Hospital. The shortest route without breaking the law is:

    A. Southwest on River Drive, right on Forest, cross Old Bridge, south on Meadow, and west on Burnt to hospital entrance.
    B. Southwest on River Drive, right on New Bridge, left on Meadow, west on Burnt to hospital entrance.
    C. Southwest on River Drive, right on Old Bridge, left on Turner, right on Burnt to hospital entrance.
    D. North on River Drive to Topp, through City Park to Forest, cross Old Bridge, left on Meadow, west on Burnt to hospital entrance.

2. After returning to the police station, the officers receive a call to pick up injured persons at an accident site (located on the east side of New Bridge) and return to Valley Hospital. The shortest route without breaking the law is:

    A. West on Roller, north on River Drive, left to accident scene at New Bridge, then north on River Drive to hospital entrance.
    B. North on Third, left on Forest, north on River Drive, left to accident scene at new Bridge, then south on River Drive to hospital entrance.
    C. East on Roller, left on First, west on Maple, north on Third, left on Forest, north on River Drive to accident scene at New Bridge, then south on River Drive to hospital entrance.
    D. North on Third, left on Forest, cross Old Bridge, north on Meadow to New Bridge, south on Meadow, east over Old Bridge, then south on River Drive to hospital entrance.

3. While at the Valley Hospital, the officers receive a call asking them to pick up materials at the Ace Supply and return them to the police station. The shortest route without breaking the law is:

    A. North on River Drive, cross New Bridge, west on Crown to Ace Supply, then south on Front, east on Burnt, north on Meadow, cross Old Bridge, east on Forest, south on Third to police station.
    B. North on River Drive, right on Roller to police station, then north on Third, left on Forest, cross Old Bridge, north on Meadow, west on Crown to Ace Supply.
    C. North on River Drive, cross Old Bridge, north on Meadow, west on Crown to Ace Supply, then east on Crown, south on Meadow, cross Old Bridge, east on Forest, south on Third to police station.
    D. North on River Drive, cross Old Bridge, south on Meadow, west on Burnt, north on Front to Ace Supply, then east on Crown, south on Meadow, cross Old Bridge, east on Forest, south on Third to police station.

KEY (CORRECT ANSWERS)

1. A
2. B
3. C

MAP READING

EXAMINATION SECTION
TEST 1

DIRECTIONS: Each question or incomplete statement is followed by several suggested answers or completions. Select the one that BEST answers the question or completes the statement. *PRINT THE LETTER OF THE CORRECT ANSWER IN THE SPACE AT THE RIGHT.*

Questions 1-3.

DIRECTIONS: Questions 1 through 3 are to be answered SOLELY on the basis of the map which appears on the next page. The flow of traffic is indicated by the arrow. If there is only one arrow shown, then traffic flows only in the direction indicated by the arrow. If there are two arrows shown, then traffic flows in both directions. You must follow the flow of traffic.

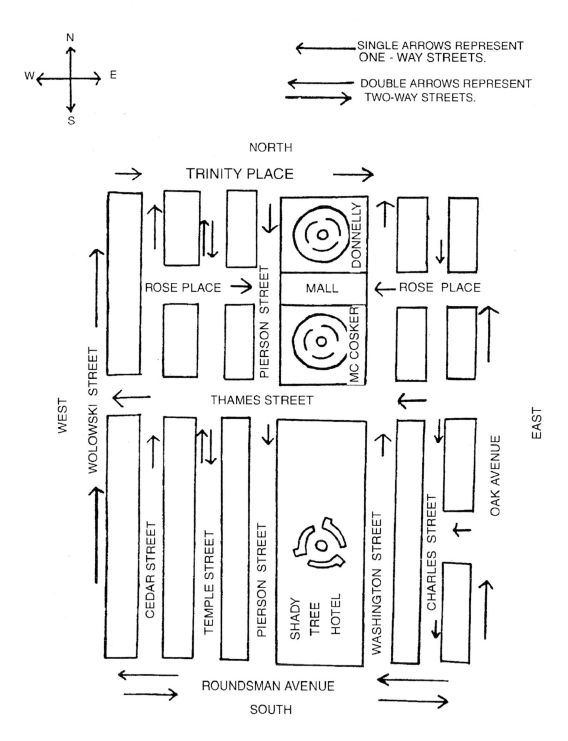

1. Police Officers Simms and O'Brien are located at Roundsman Avenue and Washington   1.____
    Street. The radio dispatcher has assigned them to investigate a motor vehicle accident at
    the corner of Pierson Street and Rose Place.
    Which one of the following is the SHORTEST route for them to take in their patrol car,
    making sure to obey all traffic regulations?
    Travel

    A. west on Roundsman Avenue, then north on Temple Street, then east on Thames
        Street, then north on Pierson Street to Rose Place
    B. east on Roundsman Avenue, then north on Oak Avenue, then west on Rose Place
        to Pierson Street
    C. west on Roundsman Avenue, then north on Temple Street, then east on Rose
        Place to Pierson Street
    D. east on Roundsman Avenue, then north on Oak Avenue, then west on Thames
        Street, then north on Temple Street, then east on Rose Place to Pierson Street

2. Police Officers Sears and Castro are located at Cedar Street and Roundsman Avenue.   2.____
    They are called to respond to the scene of a burglary at Rose Place and Charles Street.
    Which one of the following is the SHORTEST route for them to take in their patrol car,
    making sure to obey all traffic regulations?
    Travel

    A. east on Roundsman Avenue, then north on Oak Avenue, then west on Rose Place
        to Charles Street
    B. east on Roundsman Avenue, then north on Washington Street, then east on Rose
        Place to Charles Street
    C. west on Roundsman Avenue, then north on Wolowski Street, then east on Trinity
        Place, then south on Charles Street to Rose Place
    D. east on Roundsman Avenue, then north on Charles Street to Rose Place

3. Police Officer Glasser is in an unmarked car at the intersection of Rose Place and Tem-   3.____
    ple Street when he begins to follow two robbery suspects. The suspects go south for two
    blocks, then turn left for two blocks, then make another left turn for one more block. The
    suspects realize they are being followed and make a left turn and travel two more blocks
    and then make a right turn.
    In what direction are the suspects now headed?

    A. North   B. South   C. East   D. West

Questions 4-6.

DIRECTIONS: Questions 4 through 6 are to be answered SOLELY on the basis of the follow-
               ing map. The flow of traffic is indicated by the arrows. If there is only one arrow
               shown, then traffic flows only in the direction indicated by the arrow. If there are
               two arrows shown, then traffic flows in both directions. You must follow the flow
               of traffic.

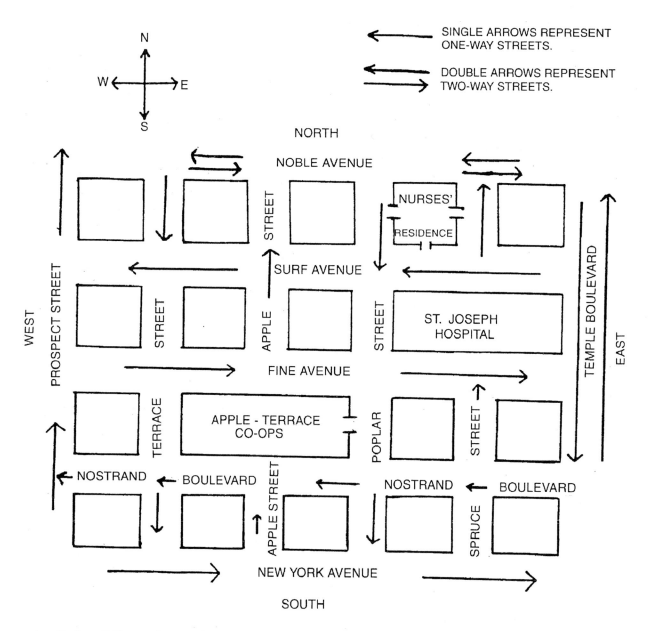

4. Police Officers Gannon and Vine are located at the intersection of Terrace Street and Surf Avenue when they receive a call from the radio dispatcher stating that they need to respond to an attempted murder at Spruce Street and Fine Avenue.
Which one of the following is the SHORTEST route for them to take in their patrol car, making sure to obey all traffic regulations?
Travel _____ to Spruce Street.   4.____

   A.   west on Surf Avenue, then north on Prospect Street, then east on Noble Avenue, then south on Poplar Street, then east on Fine Avenue
   B.   east on Surf Avenue, then south on Poplar Street, then east on Fine Avenue
   C.   west on Surf Avenue, then south on Prospect Street, then east on Fine Avenue
   D.   south on Terrace Street, then east on Fine Avenue

5. Police Officers Sears and Ronald are at Nostrand Boulevard and Prospect Street. They   5.____
   receive a call assigning them to investigate a disruptive group of youths at Temple Boulevard and Surf Avenue.
   Which one of the following is the SHORTEST route for them to take in their patrol car,
   making sure to obey all traffic regulations?
   Travel

   A. north on Prospect Street, then east on Surf Avenue to Temple Boulevard
   B. north on Prospect Street, then east on Noble Avenue, then south on Temple Boule-
      vard to Surf Avenue
   C. north on Prospect Street, then east on Fine Avenue, then north on Temple Boule-
      vard to Surf Avenue
   D. south on Prospect Street, then east on New York Avenue, then north on Temple
      Boulevard to Surf Avenue

6. While on patrol at Prospect Street and New York Avenue, Police Officers Ross and Rock   6.____
   are called to a burglary in progress near the entrance to the Apple-Terrace Co-ops on
   Poplar Street midway between Fine Avenue and Nostrand Boulevard.
   Which one of the following is the SHORTEST route for them to take in their patrol car,
   making sure to obey all traffic regulations?
   Travel _____ Poplar Street.

   A. east on New York Avenue, then north
   B. north on Prospect Avenue, then east on Fine Avenue, then south
   C. north on Prospect Street, then east on Surf Avenue, then south
   D. east on New York Avenue, then north on Temple Boulevard, then west on Surf Ave-
      nue, then south

Questions 7-8.

DIRECTIONS: Questions 7 and 8 are to be answered SOLELY on the basis of the map which
appears below. The flow of traffic is indicated by the arrows. If there is only one
arrow shown, then traffic flows only in the direction indicated by the arrow. If
there are two arrows shown, then traffic flows in both directions. You must follow the flow of traffic.

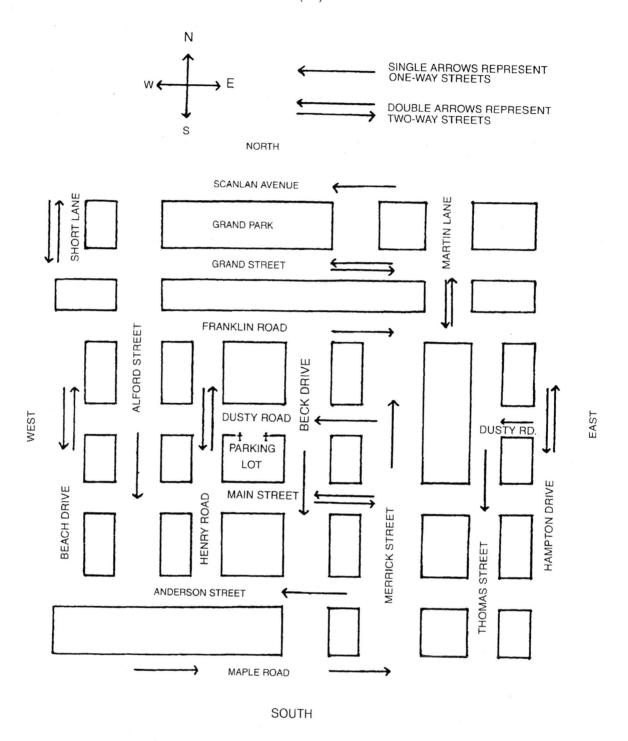

SINGLE ARROWS REPRESENT ONE-WAY STREETS

DOUBLE ARROWS REPRESENT TWO-WAY STREETS

7. Police Officers Gold and Warren are at the intersection of Maple Road and Hampton Drive. The radio dispatcher has assigned them to investigate an attempted auto theft in the parking lot on Dusty Road.

Which one of the following is the SHORTEST route for the officers to take in their patrol car to get to the entrance of the parking lot on Dusty Road, making sure to obey all traffic regulations?

Travel _____ to the parking lot entrance.

7.___

A. north on Hampton Drive, then west on Dusty Road
B. west on Maple Road, then north on Beck Drive, then west on Dusty Road
C. north on Hampton Drive, then west on Anderson Street, then north on Merrick Street, then west on Dusty Road
D. west on Maple Road, then north on Merrick Street, then west on Dusty Road

8. Police Officer Gladden is in a patrol car at the intersection of Beach Drive and Anderson Street when he spots a suspicious car. Police Officer Gladden calls the radio dispatcher to determine if the vehicle was stolen. Police Officer Gladden then follows the vehicle north on Beach Drive for three blocks, then turns right and proceeds for one block and makes another right. He then follows the vehicle for two blocks, and then they both make a left turn and continue driving. Police Officer Gladden now receives a call from the dispatcher stating the car was reported stolen and signals for the vehicle to pull to the side of the road.
In what direction was Police Officer Gladden heading at the time he signaled for the other car to pull over?

A. North   B. East   C. South   D. West

Questions 9-10.

DIRECTIONS: Questions 9 and 10 are to be answered SOLELY on the basis of the map which appears on the following page. The flow of traffic is indicated by the arrows. If there is only one arrow shown, then traffic flows only in the direction indicated by the arrow. If there are two arrows shown, then traffic flows in both directions. You must follow the flow of traffic.

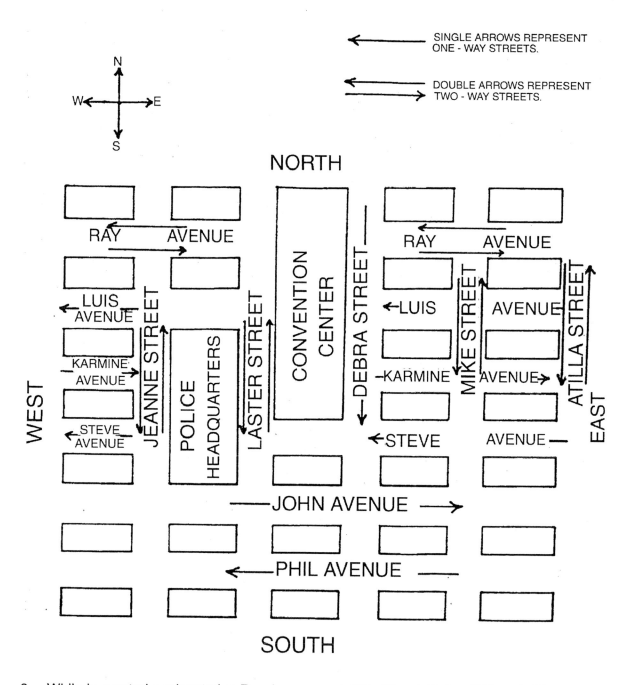

SINGLE ARROWS REPRESENT ONE - WAY STREETS.

DOUBLE ARROWS REPRESENT TWO - WAY STREETS.

9. While in a patrol car located at Ray Avenue and Atilla Street, Police Officer Ashley receives a call from the dispatcher to respond to an assault at Jeanne Street and Karmine Avenue.
Which one of the following is the SHORTEST route for Officer Ashley to follow in his patrol car, making sure to obey all traffic regulations?
Travel

9.____

   A.   south on Atilla Street, west on Luis Avenue, south on Debra Street, west on Steve Avenue, north on Lester Street, west on Luis Avenue, then one block south on Jeanne Street

   B.   south on Atilla Street, then four blocks west on Phil Avenue, then north on Jeanne Street to Karmine Avenue

    C.   west on Ray Avenue to Debra Street, then five blocks south to Phil Avenue, then west to Jeanne Street, then three blocks north to Karmine Avenue

    D.   south on Atilla Street, then four blocks west on John Avenue, then north on Jeanne Street to Karmine Avenue

10.   After taking a complaint report from the assault victim, Officer Ashley receives a call from the dispatcher to respond to an auto larceny in progress at the corner of Debra Street and Luis Avenue.   10.____

Which one of the following is the SHORTEST route for Officer Ashley to follow in his patrol car, making sure to obey all traffic regulations?

Travel

    A.   south on Jeanne Street to John Avenue, then east three blocks on John Avenue, then north on Mike Street to Luis Avenue, then west to Debra Street

    B.   south on Jeanne Street to John Avenue, then east two blocks on John Avenue, then north on Debra Street to Luis Avenue

    C.   north on Jeanne Street two blocks, then east on Ray Avenue for one block, then south on Lester Street to Steve Avenue, then one block east on Steve Avenue, then north on Debra Street to Luis Avenue

    D.   south on Jeanne Street to John Avenue, then east on John Avenue to Atilla Street, then north three blocks to Luis Avenue, then west to Debra Street

Questions 11-13.

DIRECTIONS: Questions 11 through 13 are to be answered SOLELY on the basis of the following map. The flow of traffic is indicated by the arrows. You must follow the flow of traffic.

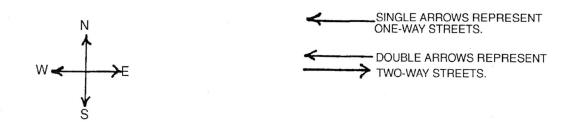

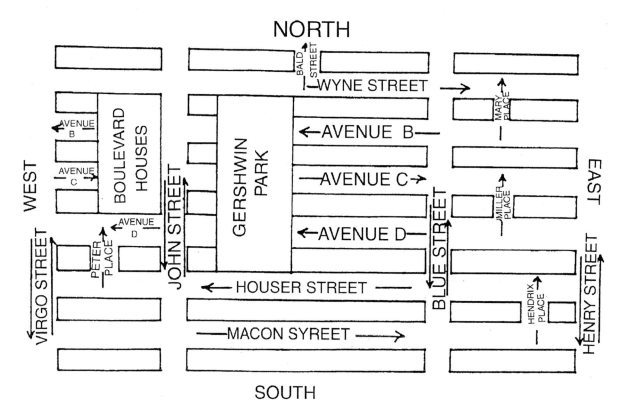

11. Police Officers Ranking and Fish are located at Wyne Street and John Street. The radio   11.____
dispatcher has assigned them to investigate a motor vehicle accident at the corner of
Henry Street and Houser Street.
Which one of the following is the SHORTEST route for them to take in their patrol car,
making sure to obey all traffic regulations?
Travel

    A. four blocks south on John Street, then three blocks east on Houser Street to Henry
       Street
    B. two blocks east on Wyne Street, then two blocks south on Blue Street, then two
       blocks east on Avenue C, then two blocks south on Henry Street
    C. two blocks east on Wyne Street, then five blocks south on Blue Street, then two
       blocks east on Macon Street, then one block north on Henry Street
    D. five blocks south on John Street, then three blocks east on Macon Street, then one
       block north to Houser Street

12. Police Officers Rizzo and Latimer are located at Avenue B and Virgo Street. They respond to the scene of a robbery at Miller Place and Avenue D.
Which one of the following is the SHORTEST route for them to take in their patrol car, making sure to obey all traffic regulations?
Travel _____ to Miller Place.

12.____

   A. one block north on Virgo Street, then four blocks east on Wyne Street, then three blocks south on Henry Street, then one block west on Avenue D
   B. four blocks south on Virgo Street, then two blocks east on Macon Street, then two blocks north on Blue Street, then one block east on Avenue D
   C. three blocks south on Virgo Street, then east on Houser Street to Henry Street, then one block north on Henry Street, then one block west on Avenue D
   D. four blocks south on Virgo Street, then four blocks east to Henry Street, then north to Avenue D, then one block west

13. Police Officer Bendix is in an unmarked patrol car at the intersection of John Street and Macon Street when he begins to follow a robbery suspect. The suspect goes one block east, turns left, travels for three blocks, and then turns right. He drives for two blocks and then makes a right turn. In the middle of the block, the suspect realizes he is being followed and makes a u-turn. In what direction is the suspect now headed?

13.____

   A. North   B. South   C. East   D. West

Questions 14-15.

DIRECTIONS: Questions 14 and 15 are to be answered SOLELY on the basis of the following map. The flow of traffic is indicated by the arrows. If there is only one arrow shown, then traffic flows only in the direction indicated by the arrow. If there are two arrows shown, then traffic flows in both directions. You must follow the flow of traffic.

NORTH

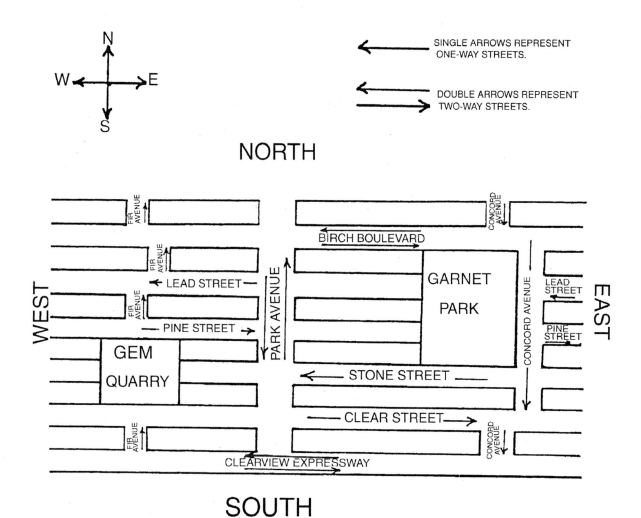

SOUTH

14. You are located at Fir Avenue and Birch Boulevard and receive a request to respond to a   14.____
disturbance at Fir Avenue and Clear Street.
Which one of the following is the MOST direct route for you to take in your patrol car,
making sure to obey all traffic regulations?
Travel

    A. one block east on Birch Boulevard, then four blocks south on Park Avenue, then
one block east on Clear Street

    B. two blocks east on Birch Boulevard, then three blocks south on Concord Avenue,
then two blocks west on Stone Street, then one block south on Park Avenue, then
one block west on Clear Street

    C. one block east on Birch Boulevard, then five blocks south on Park Avenue, then
one block west on the Clearview Expressway, then one block north on Fir Avenue

    D. two blocks south on Fir Avenue, then one block east on Pine Street, then three
blocks south on Park Avenue, then one block east on the Clearview Expressway,
then one block north on Fir Avenue

15. You are located at the Clearview Expressway and Concord Avenue and receive a call to respond to a crime in progress at Concord Avenue and Pine Street. Which one of the following is the MOST direct route for you to take in your patrol car, making sure to obey all traffic regulations?
Travel

    A. two blocks west on the Clearview Expressway, then one block north on Fir Avenue, then one block east on Clear Street, then four blocks north on Park Avenue, then one block east on Birch Boulevard, then two blocks south on Concord Avenue

    B. one block north on Concord Avenue, then one block west on Clear Street, then one block north on Park Avenue, then one block east on Stone Street, then one block north on Concord Avenue

    C. one block west on the Clearview Expressway, then four blocks north on Park Avenue, then one block west on Lead Street, then one block south on Fir Avenue

    D. one block west on the Clearview Expressway, then five blocks north on Park Avenue, then one block east on Birch Boulevard, then two blocks south on Concord Avenue

15.____

Questions 16-20.

DIRECTIONS: Questions 16 through 20 are to be answered SOLELY on the basis of the following map. The flow of traffic is indicated by the arrows. You must follow the flow of traffic.

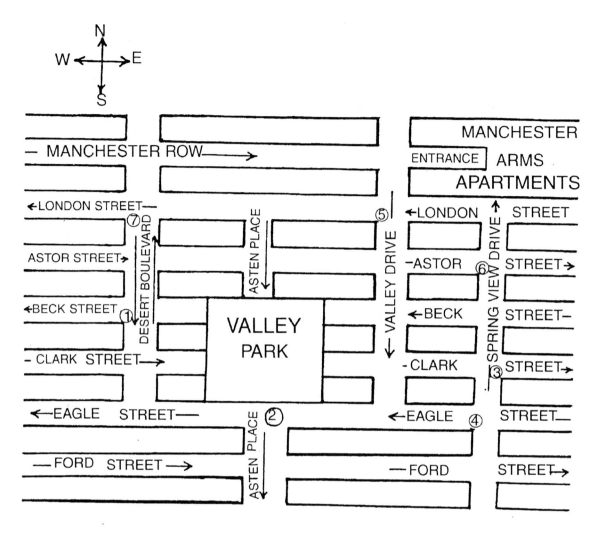

16. If you are located at Point 7 and travel south for one block, then turn east and travel two blocks, then turn south and travel two blocks, then turn east and travel one block, you will be CLOSEST to Point

16.___

   A. 2   B. 3   C. 4   D. 6

17. If you are located at Point 3 and travel north for one block, and then turn west and travel one block, and then turn south and travel two blocks, and then turn west and travel one block, you will be CLOSEST to Point

17.___

   A. 1   B. 2   C. 4   D. 6

18. You are located at Astor Street and Spring View Drive. You receive a call of a crime in progress at the intersection of Beck Street and Desert Boulevard.
Which one of the following is the MOST direct route for you to take in your patrol car, making sure to obey all traffic regulations?
Travel

18.___

   A. one block north on Spring View Drive, then three blocks west on London Street, then two blocks south on Desert Boulevard

   B. three blocks west on Astor Street, then one block south on Desert Boulevard

C. one block south on Spring View Drive, then three blocks west on Beck Street
D. three blocks south on Spring View Drive, then three blocks west on Eagle Street, then two blocks north on Desert Boulevard

19. You are located on Clark Street and Desert Boulevard and must respond to a distur-   19.____
    bance at Clark Street and Spring View Drive.
    Which one of the following is the MOST direct route for you to take in your patrol car, making sure to obey all traffic regulations?
    Travel

    A. two blocks north on Desert Boulevard, then three blocks east on Astor Street, then two blocks south on Spring View Drive
    B. one block south on Desert Boulevard, then three blocks east on Eagle Street, then one block north on Spring View Drive
    C. two blocks north on Desert Boulevard, then two blocks east on Astor Street, then three blocks south on Valley Drive, then one block east on Eagle Street, then one block north on Spring View Drive
    D. two blocks north on Desert Boulevard, then two blocks east on Astor Street, then two blocks south on Valley Drive, then one block east on Clark Street

20. You are located at Valley Drive and Beck Street and receive a call to respond to the cor-   20.____
    ner of Asten Place and Astor Street.
    Which one of the following is the MOST direct route for you to take in your patrol car, making sure to obey all traffic regulations?
    Travel _____ on Astor Street.

    A. one block north on Valley Drive, then one block west
    B. two blocks south on Valley Drive, then one block east on Eagle Street, then three blocks north on Spring View Drive, then two blocks west
    C. two blocks south on Valley Drive, then two blocks west on Eagle Street, then three blocks north on Desert Boulevard, then one block east
    D. one block south on Valley Drive, then one block east on Clark Street, then two blocks north on Spring View Drive, then two blocks west

---

KEY (CORRECT ANSWERS)

1.	C	11.	B
2.	A	12.	A
3.	A	13.	A
4.	D	14.	C
5.	C	15.	D
6.	B	16.	B
7.	C	17.	B
8.	B	18.	A
9.	A	19.	D
10.	A	20.	C

READING COMPREHENSION
UNDERSTANDING AND INTERPRETING WRITTEN MATERIAL
EXAMINATION SECTION
TEST 1

DIRECTIONS: Each question or incomplete statement is followed by several suggested answers or completions. Select the one that BEST answers the question or completes the statement. *PRINT THE LETTER OF THE CORRECT ANSWER IN THE SPACE AT THE RIGHT.*

Questions 1-4.

DIRECTIONS: Questions 1 through 4 are to be answered SOLELY on the basis of the information given in the paragraph below.

Abandoned cars – with tires gone, chrome stripped away, and windows smashed – have become a common sight on the city's streets. In 2000, more than 72,000 were deposited at curbs by owners who never came back, an increase of 15,000 from the year before and more than 30 times the number abandoned a decade ago. In January 2001, the city Environmental Protection Administrator asked the State Legislature to pass a law requiring a buyer of a new automobile to deposit $100 and an owner of an automobile at the time the law takes effect to deposit $50 with the State Department of Motor Vehicles. In return, they would be given a certificate of deposit which would be passed on to each succeeding owner. The final owner would get the deposit money back if he could present proof that he has disposed of his car *in an environmentally acceptable manner.* The Legislature has given no indication that it plans to rush ahead on the matter.

1. The number of cars abandoned in the city streets in 1990 was MOST NEARLY   1.____

   A. 2,500   B. 12,000   C. 27,500   D. 57,000

2. The proposed law would require a person who owned a car bought before the law was passed to deposit   2.____

   A. $100 with the State Department of Motor Vehicles
   B. $50 with the Environmental Protection Administration
   C. $100 with the State Legislature
   D. $50 with the State Department of Motor Vehicles

3. The proposed law would require the State to return the deposit money ONLY when the   3.____

   A. original owner of the car shows proof that he sold it
   B. last owner of the car shows proof that he got rid of the car in a satisfactory way
   C. owner of a car shows proof that he has transferred the certificate of deposit to the next owner
   D. last owner of a car returns the certificate of deposit

4. The MAIN idea or theme of the above article is that   4.___

    A. a proposed new law would make it necessary for car owners in the State to pay additional taxes
    B. the State Legislature is against a proposed law to require deposits from automobile owners to prevent them from abandoning their cars
    C. the city is trying to find a solution for the increasing number of cars abandoned on its streets
    D. to pay for the removal of abandoned cars the city's Environmental Protection Administrator has asked the State to fine automobile owners who abandon their vehicles

Questions 5-7.

DIRECTIONS: Questions 5 through 7 are to be answered SOLELY on the basis of the information given in the paragraph below.

    The regulations applying to parking meters provide that the driver is required to deposit the appropriate coin immediately upon parking and it is illegal for him to return at a later period to extend the parking time. If there is unused time on a parking meter, another car may be parked for a period not to exceed the unused time without the deposit of a coin. Operators of commercial vehicles are not required to deposit coins while loading or unloading expeditiously. By definition, a vehicle is considered parked even though there is a driver at the wheel and the meter must be used by the driver of such car.

5. According to the above paragraph, the regulations applying to parking meters do NOT   5.___

    A. allow the driver of a parked vehicle to stay in his car
    B. consider any loading or unloading of a vehicle as parking
    C. make any distinction between an unoccupied car and one with the driver at the wheel
    D. permit a driver who has parked a car at a meter with unused parking time to put a coin in the meter

6. According to the above paragraph, it is a violation of the parking meter regulations to   6.___

    A. load and unload slowly
    B. park commercial vehicles except for loading and unloading
    C. put a second coin in the meter in order to park longer
    D. use a parking space at any time without depositing a coin

7. The above paragraph CLEARLY indicates   7.___

    A. the number of minutes a vehicle may be parked
    B. the value of the coin that is to be put in the meter
    C. what is meant by a commercial vehicle
    D. when a car may be parked free

Questions 8-13.

DIRECTIONS: Questions 8 through 13 are to be answered on the basis of the information given in the paragraph below.

There are many types of reports. One of these is the field report, which requests information specified and grouped under columns or headings. A detailed, printed form is often used in submitting field reports. However, these printed, standardized forms provide a limited amount of space. The field man is required to make the decision as to how much of the information he has should go directly into the report and how much should be left for clarification if and when he is called in to explain a reported finding. In many instances, the addition of a short explanation of the finding might relieve the reader of the report of the necessity to seek an explanation. Therefore, the basic factual information asked for by the printed report form should often be clarified by some simple explanatory statement. If this is done, the reported finding becomes meaningful to the reader of the report who is far from the scene of the subject matter dealt with in the report. The significance of that which is reported finds its expression in the adoption of certain policies, improvements, or additions essential to furthering the effectiveness of the program.

8.   According to the above paragraph, the field report asks for   8._____

   A.   a detailed statement of the facts
   B.   field information which comes under the heading of technical data
   C.   replies to well-planned questions
   D.   specific information in different columns

9.   According to the above paragraph, the usual printed field report form   9._____

   A.   does not have much room for writing
   B.   is carefully laid out
   C.   is necessary for the collection of facts
   D.   usually has from three to four columns

10.   According to the above paragraph, the man in the field MUST decide if   10._____

   A.   a report is needed at all
   B.   he should be called in to explain a reported finding
   C.   he should put all the information he has into the report
   D.   the reader of the report is justified in seeking an explanation

11.   According to the above paragraph, the man in the field may be required to   11._____

   A.   be acquainted with the person or persons who will read his report
   B.   explain the information he reports
   C.   give advice on specific problems
   D.   keep records of the amount of work he completes

12.   According to the above paragraph, the value of an explanatory statement added to the factual information reported in the printed forms is that it   12._____

   A.   allows the person making the report to express himself briefly
   B.   forces the person making the report to think logically
   C.   helps the report reader understand the facts reported
   D.   makes it possible to turn in the report later

13. According to the above paragraph, the importance of the information given by the field man in his report is shown by the 13.___

 A. adoption of policies and improvements
 B. effectiveness of the field staff
 C. fact that such a report is required
 D. necessary cost studies to back up the facts

Questions 14-15.

DIRECTIONS: Questions 14 and 15 are to be answered on the basis of the information contained in the following paragraph.

The driver of the collection crew shall at all times remain in or on a department vehicle in which there is revenue. In the event such driver must leave the vehicle, he shall designate one of the other members of the crew to remain in or on the vehicle. The member of the crew so designated by the driver shall remain in or on the vehicle until relieved by the driver or another member of the crew. The vehicle may be left unattended only when there is no revenue contained therein provided, however, that in that event the vehicle shall be locked. The loss of any vehicle or any of its contents, including revenue, resulting from any deviation from this rule, shall be the responsibility of the member or members of crew who shall be guilty of such deviation.

14. The vehicle of a collection crew may be left with no one in it only if 14.___

 A. it is locked
 B. there is a crew member nearby
 C. there is no money in it
 D. there is only one member in the crew

15. If money is stolen from an unattended vehicle of a collection crew, the employee held responsible is the 15.___

 A. driver
 B. one who left the vehicle unattended
 C. one who left the vehicle unlocked
 D. one who relieved the driver

Questions 16-18.

DIRECTIONS: Questions 16 through 18 are to be answered SOLELY on the basis of the information given in the paragraph below.

Safety belts provide protection for the passengers of a vehicle by preventing them from crashing around inside if the vehicle is involved in a collision. They operate on the principle similar to that used in the packaging of fragile items. You become a part of the vehicle package, and you are kept from being tossed about inside if the vehicle is suddenly decelerated. Many injury-causing collisions at low speeds, for example at city intersections, could have been injury-free if the occupants had fastened their safety belts. There is a double advantage to the driver in that it not only protects him from harm, but prevents him from being yanked away from the wheel, thereby permitting him to maintain control of the car.

16. The principle on which seat belts work is that 16.____

    A. a car and its driver and passengers are fragile
    B. a person fastened to the car will not be thrown around when the car slows down suddenly
    C. the driver and passengers of a car that is suddenly decelerated will be thrown forward
    D. the driver and passengers of an automobile should be packaged the way fragile items are packaged

17. We can assume from the above passage that safety belts should be worn at all times because you can never tell when 17.____

    A. a car will be forced to turn off onto another road
    B. it will be necessary to shift into low gear to go up a hill
    C. you will have to speed up to pass another car
    D. a car may have to come to a sudden stop

18. Besides preventing injury, an ADDITIONAL benefit from the use of safety belts is that 18.____

    A. collisions are fewer
    B. damage to the car is kept down
    C. the car can be kept under control
    D. the number of accidents at city intersections is reduced

Questions 19-24.

DIRECTIONS: Questions 19 through 24 are to be answered on the basis of the following reading passage covering Procedures For Patrol.

PROCEDURES FOR PATROL

The primary function of all Parking Enforcement Agents assigned to patrol duty shall be to patrol assigned areas and issue summonses to violators of various sections of the City Traffic Regulations, which sections govern the parking or operation of vehicles. Parking Enforcement Agents occasionally may be called upon to distribute educational pamphlets and perform other work, at the discretion of the Bureau Chief.

Each Agent on patrol duty will be assigned a certain area (or areas) to be patrolled each day. These areas will be assigned during the daily roll call. Walking Cards will describe the street locations of the patrol and the manner in which the patrol is to be walked.

A Traffic Department vehicle will be provided for daily patrol assignments when necessary.

Each Agent shall accomplish an assigned field patrol in the following manner:

    a. Start each patrol at the location specified on the daily patrol sheet, and proceed as per walking instructions.
    b. Approach each metered space being utilized (each metered space in which a vehicle is parked). If the meter shows the expired flag, the member of the force shall prepare and affix a summons to the vehicle parked at meter.

c. Any vehicle in violation of any regulation governing the parking, standing, stopping, or movement of vehicles will be issued a summons.
d. No summons will be issued to a vehicle displaying an authorized vehicle identification plate of the Police Department unless the vehicle is parked in violation of the No Standing, No Stopping, Hydrant, Bus Stop, or Double Parking Regulations. Identification plates for Police Department automobiles are made of plastic and are of rectangular shape, 10 3/4" long, 3 3/4" high, black letters and numerals on a white background. The words *POLICE DEPT.* are printed on the face with the identification number. Identification plates for private automobiles are the same size and shape as those used on Police Department automobiles.

An Agent on patrol, when observing a person *feeding* a street meter (placing an additional coin in a meter so as to leave the vehicle parked for an additional period) shall prepare and affix a summons to the vehicle.

An Agent on patrol shall note on a computer card each missing or defective, out of order, or otherwise damaged meter.

19. Of the following, the work which the Parking Enforcement Agent performs MOST often is   19.___

    A. issuing summonses for parking violations
    B. distributing educational pamphlets
    C. assisting the Bureau Chief
    D. driving a city vehicle

20. The area to be covered by a Parking Enforcement Agent on patrol is   20.___

    A. determined by the Police Department
    B. regulated by the city Traffic Regulations
    C. marked off with red flags
    D. described on Walking Cards

21. A Parking Enforcement Agent reports a broken meter by   21.___

    A. issuing a summons
    B. making a mark on a computer card
    C. raising the flag on the broken meter
    D. attending a daily roll call

22. With respect to the use of an automobile for patrol duty,   22.___

    A. Parking Enforcement Agents must supply their own cars for patrol
    B. automobiles for patrol will be supplied by the Police Department
    C. Parking Enforcement Agents are permitted to park in a bus stop
    D. department vehicles will be provided when required for patrol

23. Parking Enforcement Agents sometimes issue summonses to drivers for *feeding* a street   23.___
meter in violation of parking regulations.
Which one of the following situations describes such a violation?
A driver

    A. has moved from one metered space to another
    B. has parked next to a Police Department No Standing sign
    C. is parked by a meter which shows 30 minutes time still remaining
    D. has used a coin to reset the meter after his first time period expired

24. Vehicles displaying an authorized vehicle identification plate of the Police Department   24.____
are allowed to park at expired meters.
Which one of the following statements describes the proper size of identification plates
for private automobiles used for police work?
They

    A.   are 10 3/4" long and 3 3/4" high
    B.   have white letters and numerals on a black background
    C.   are 3 3/4" long and 10 3/4" high
    D.   have black letters and numerals on a white background

Questions 25-30.

DIRECTIONS: Questions 25 through 30 are to be answered on the basis of the following
reading passage covering the Operation of Department Motor Vehicles.

OPERATION OF DEPARTMENT MOTOR VEHICLES

When operating a Traffic Department motor vehicle, a member of the force must show
every courtesy to other drivers, obey all traffic signs and traffic regulations, obey all other law-
ful authority, and handle the vehicle in a manner which will foster safety practices in others
and create a favorable impression of the Bureau, the Department, and the City. The operator
and passengers MUST use the safety belts.

Driving Rules

    a.   DO NOT operate a mechanically defective vehicle.
        DO NOT race engine on starting.
        DO NOT tamper with mechanical equipment.
        DO NOT run engine if there is an indication of low engine oil pressure, overheating,
        or no transmission oil.

    b.   When parking on highway, all safety precautions must be observed.

    c.   When parking in a garage or parking field, observe a maximum speed of 5 miles
        per hour. Place shift lever in park or neutral position, effectively apply hand brake,
        then shut off all ignition and light switches to prevent excess battery drain, and
        close all windows.

Reporting Defects

    a.   Report all observed defects on Drivers' Vehicle Defect Card and on Monthly Vehi-
        cle Report Form 49 in sufficient detail so a mechanic can easily locate the source
        of trouble.
    b.   Enter vehicle road service calls and actual time of occurrence on Monthly Vehicle
        Report.

Reporting Accidents

Promptly report all facts of each accident as follows: For serious accidents, including those involving personal injury, call your supervisor as soon as possible. Give all the appropriate information about the accident to your supervisor. Record vehicle registration information, including the name of the registered owner, the state, year, and serial number, and the classification marking on the license plates. Also record the operator's license number and other identifying information, and, if it applies, the injured person's age and sex. Give a full description of how the accident happened, and what happened following the accident, including the vehicles in collision, witnesses, police badge number, hospital, condition of road surface, time of day, weather conditions, location (near, far, center of intersection), and damage.

Repairs to Automobiles

When a Department motor vehicle requires repairs that cannot be made by the operator, or requires replacement of parts or accessories (including tires and tubes), or requires towing, the operator shall notify the District Commander.

When a Departmental motor vehicle is placed out of service for repairs, the Regional Commander shall assign another vehicle, if available.

Daily Operator's Report

The operator of a Department automobile shall keep a daily maintenance record of the vehicle, and note any unusual occurrences, on the Daily Operator's Report.

25. Parking Enforcement Agents who are assigned to operate Department motor vehicles on patrol are expected to   25.___

    A. disregard the posted speed limits to save time
    B. remove their seat belts on short trips
    C. show courtesy to other drivers on the road
    D. take the right of way at all intersections

26. The driver of a Department motor vehicle should   26.___

    A. leave the windows open when parking the vehicle in a garage
    B. drive the vehicle at approximately 10 miles per hour in a parking field
    C. be alert for indication of low engine oil pressure and overheated engine
    D. start a cold vehicle by racing the engine for 5 minutes

27. The reason that all defects on a Department vehicle that have been observed by its driver should be noted on a Monthly Vehicle Report Form 49 is: 27.___

    A. This action will foster better safety practices among other Agents
    B. The source of the defect may be located easily by a trained mechanic
    C. All the facts of an accident will be reported promptly
    D. The District Commander will not have to make road calls

28. If the driver of a Department vehicle is involved in an accident, an Accident Report should be made out. This Report should include a full description of how the accident happened.
Which of the following statements would PROPERLY belong in an Accident Report?

   A. The accident occurred at the intersection of Broadway and 42nd Street.
   B. The operator of the Department motor vehicle replaced the windshield wiper.
   C. The vehicle was checked for gas and water before the patrol began.
   D. A bus passed two parked vehicles.

28.____

29. When a Department vehicle is disabled, whom should the operator notify? The

   A. Traffic Department garage
   B. Assistant Bureau Chief
   C. Police Department
   D. District Commander

29.____

30. The PROPER way for an operator of a Department vehicle to report unusual occurrences with respect to the operation of the vehicle is to

   A. follow the same procedures as for reporting a defect
   B. request the Regional Commander to assign another vehicle
   C. phone the Bureau Chief as soon as possible
   D. make a note of the circumstances on the Daily Operator's Report

30.____

KEY (CORRECT ANSWERS)

1.	A	16.	B
2.	D	17.	D
3.	B	18.	C
4.	C	19.	A
5.	C	20.	D
6.	C	21.	B
7.	D	22.	D
8.	D	23.	D
9.	A	24.	A
10.	C	25.	C
11.	B	26.	C
12.	C	27.	B
13.	A	28.	A
14.	C	29.	D
15.	B	30.	D

TEST 2

DIRECTIONS: Each question or incomplete statement is followed by several suggested answers or completions. Select the one that BEST answers the question or completes the statement. *PRINT THE LETTER OF THE CORRECT ANSWER IN THE SPACE AT THE RIGHT.*

Questions 1-4.

DIRECTIONS: Questions 1 through 4 are to be answered SOLELY on the basis of the information contained in the following passage.

Of those arrested in the city in 2003 for felonies or misdemeanors, only 32% were found guilty of any charge. Fifty-six percent of such arrestees were acquitted or had their cases dismissed. 11% failed to appear for trial, and 1% received other dispositions. Of those found guilty, only 7.4% received any sentences of over one year in jail. Only 50% of those found guilty were sentenced to any further time in jail. When considered with the low probability of arrests for most crimes, these figures make it clear that the crime control system in the city poses little threat to the average criminal. Delay compounds the problem. The average case took four appearances for disposition after arraignment. Twenty percent of all cases took eight or more appearances to reach a disposition. Forty-four percent of all cases took more than one year to disposition.

1. According to the above passage, crime statistics for 2003 indicate that   1.___

   A. there is a low probability of arrests for all crimes in the city
   B. the average criminal has much to fear from the law in the city
   C. over 10% of arrestees in the city charged with felonies or misdemeanors did not show up for trial
   D. criminals in the city are less likely to be caught than criminals in the rest of the country

2. The percentage of those arrested in 2003 who received sentences of over one year in jail amounted to MOST NEARLY   2.___

   A. .237   B. 2.4   C. 23.7   D. 24.0

3. According to the above passage, the percentage of arrestees in 2003 who were found guilty was   3.___

   A. 20% of those arrested for misdemeanors
   B. 11% of those arrested for felonies
   C. 50% of those sentenced to further time in jail
   D. 32% of those arrested for felonies or misdemeanors

4. According to the above paragraph, the number of appearances after arraignment and before disposition amounted to   4.___

   A. an average of four
   B. eight or more in 44% of the cases
   C. over four for cases which took more than a year
   D. between four and eight for most cases

Questions 5-6.

DIRECTIONS: Questions 5 and 6 are to be answered on the basis of the following paragraph.

A person who, with the intent to deprive or defraud another of the use and benefit of property or to appropriate the same to the use of the taker, or of any other person other than the true owner, wrongfully takes, obtains or withholds, by any means whatever, from the possession of the true owner or of any other person any money, personal property, thing in action, evidence of debt or contract, or article of value of any kind, steals such property and is guilty of larceny.

5. This definition from the Penal Law has NO application to the act of 5.____

    A.   fraudulent conversion by a vendor of city sales tax money collected from purchasers
    B.   refusing to give proper change after a purchaser has paid for an article in cash
    C.   receiving property stolen from the rightful owner
    D.   embezzling money from the rightful owner

6. According to the above paragraph, an auto mechanic who claimed to have a lien on an automobile for completed repairs and refused to surrender possession until the bill was paid 6.____

    A.   *cannot* be charged with larceny because his repairs increased the value of the car
    B.   *can* be charged with larceny because such actual possession can be construed to include intent to deprive the owner of use of the car
    C.   *cannot* be charged with larceny because the withholding is temporary and such possession is not an evidence of debt
    D.   *cannot* be charged with larceny because intent to defraud is lacking

Questions 7-12.

DIRECTIONS: Questions 7 through 12 are to be answered on the basis of the information given in the passage below. Assume that all questions refer to the same state described in the passage.

The courts and the police consider an *offense* as any conduct that is punishable by a fine or imprisonment. Such offenses include many kinds of acts—from behavior that is merely annoying, like throwing a noisy party that keeps everyone awake, all the way up to violent acts like murder. The law classifies offenses according to the penalties that are provided for them. In one state, minor offenses are called *violations*. A violation is punishable by a fine of not more than $250 or imprisonment of not more than 15 days, or both. The annoying behavior mentioned above is an example of a violation. More serious offenses are classified as *crimes*. Crimes are classified by the kind of penalty that is provided. A *misdemeanor* is a crime that is punishable by a fine of not more than $1,000 or by imprisonment of not more than 1 year, or both. Examples of misdemeanors include stealing something with a value of $100 or less, turning in a false alarm, or illegally possessing less than 1/8 of an ounce of a dangerous drug. A *felony* is a criminal offense punishable by imprisonment of more than 1 year. Murder is clearly a felony.

7. According to the above passage, any act that is punishable by imprisonment or by a fine   7.____
   is called a(n)

   A. offense   B. violation   C. crime   D. felony

8. According to the above passage, which of the following is classified as a crime?   8.____

   A. Offense punishable by 15 days imprisonment
   B. Minor offense
   C. Violation
   D. Misdemeanor

9. According to the above passage, if a person guilty of burglary can receive a prison sen-   9.____
   tence of 7 years or more, burglary would be classified as a

   A. violation   B. misdemeanor
   C. felony   D. violent act

10. According to the above passage, two offenses that would BOTH be classified as misde-   10.____
    meanors are

    A. making unreasonable noise, and stealing a $90 bicycle
    B. stealing a $75 radio, and possessing 1/16 of an ounce of heroin
    C. holding up a bank, and possessing 1/4 of a pound of marijuana
    D. falsely reporting a fire, and illegally double-parking

11. The above passage says that offenses are classified according to the penalties provided   11.____
    for them.
    On the basis of clues in the passage, who probably decides what the maximum penal-
    ties should be for the different kinds of offenses?

    A. The State lawmakers   B. The City police
    C. The Mayor   D. Officials in Washington, D.C.

12. Of the following, which BEST describes the subject matter of the passage?   12.____

    A. How society deals with criminals
    B. How offenses are classified
    C. Three types of criminal behavior
    D. The police approach to offenders

Questions 13-20.

DIRECTIONS: Questions 13 through 20 are to be answered SOLELY on the basis of the fol-
              lowing passage.

Auto theft is prevalent and costly. In 2005, 486,000 autos valued at over $500 million were stolen. About 28 percent of the inhabitants of Federal prisons are there as a result of conviction of interstate auto theft under the Dyer Act. In California alone, auto thefts cost the criminal justice system approximately $60 million yearly.

The great majority of auto theft is for temporary use rather than resale, as evidenced by the fact that 88 percent of autos stolen in 2005 were recovered. In Los Angeles, 64 percent of stolen autos that were recovered were found within two days, and about 80 percent within a week. Chicago reports that 71 percent of the recovered autos were found within four miles of the point of theft. The FBI estimates that 8 percent of stolen cars are taken for the purpose of stripping them for parts, 12 percent for resale, and 5 percent for use in another crime. Auto thefts are primarily juvenile acts. Although only 21 percent of all arrests for nontraffic offenses in 2005 were of individuals under 18 years of age, 63 percent of auto theft arrests were of persons under 18. Auto theft represents the start of many criminal careers; in an FBI sample of juvenile auto theft offenders, 41 percent had no prior arrest record.

13. In the above passage, the discussion of the reasons for auto theft does NOT include the percent of   13.____

    A.   autos stolen by prior offenders
    B.   recovered stolen autos found close to the point of theft
    C.   stolen autos recovered within a week
    D.   stolen autos which were recovered

14. Assuming the figures in the above passage remain constant, you may logically estimate the cost of auto thefts to the California criminal justice system over a five-year period beginning in 2005 to have been about _____ million.   14.____

    A. $200   B. $300   C. $440   D. $500

15. According to the above passage, the percent of stolen autos in Los Angeles which were not recovered within a week was _____ percent.   15.____

    A.   12   B.   20   C.   29   D.   36

16. According to the above passage, MOST auto thefts are committed by   16.____

    A.   former inmates of Federal prisons   B.   juveniles
    C.   persons with a prior arrest record   D.   residents of large cities

17. According to the above passage, MOST autos are stolen for   17.____

    A.   resale   B.   stripping of parts
    C.   temporary use   D.   use in another crime

18. According to the above passage, the percent of persons arrested for auto theft who were under 18   18.____

    A.   equals nearly the same percent of stolen autos which were recovered
    B.   equals nearly two-thirds of the total number of persons arrested for nontraffic offenses
    C.   is the same as the percent of persons arrested for nontraffic offenses who were under 18
    D.   is three times the percent of persons arrested for nontraffic offenses who were under 18

19. An APPROPRIATE title for the above passage is   19.____

    A.   HOW CRIMINAL CAREERS BEGIN
    B.   RECOVERY OF STOLEN CARS
    C.   SOME STATISTICS ON AUTO THEFT
    D.   THE COSTS OF AUTO THEFT

20. Based on the above passage, the number of cars taken for use in another crime in 2005 was

    A. 24,300   B. 38,880   C. 48,600   D. 58,320

20.__

Questions 21-22.

DIRECTIONS: Questions 21 and 22 are to be answered SOLELY on the basis of the following paragraph.

    If the second or third felony is such that, upon a first conviction, the offender would be punishable by imprisonment for any term less than his natural life, then such person must be sentenced to imprisonment for an indeterminate term, the minimum of which shall be not less than one-half of the longest term prescribed upon a first conviction, and the maximum of which shall be not longer than twice such longest term, provided, however, that the minimum sentence imposed hereunder upon such second or third felony offender shall in no case be less than five years; except that where the maximum punishment for a second or third felony offender hereunder is five years or less, the minimum sentence must be not less than two years.

21. According to the above paragraph, a person who has a second felony conviction shall receive as a sentence for that second felony an indeterminate term

    A. not less than twice the minimum term prescribed upon a first conviction as a maximum
    B. not less than one-half the maximum term of his first conviction as a minimum
    C. not more than twice the minimum term prescribed upon a first conviction as a minimum
    D. with a maximum of not more than twice the longest term prescribed for a first conviction for this crime

21.__

22. According to the above paragraph, if the term for this crime for a first offender is up to three years, the possible indeterminate term for this crime as a second or third felony shall have a _____ of not _____ than _____ years.

    A. minimum; less; five
    B. maximum; more; five
    C. minimum; less; one and one-half
    D. maximum; less; six

22.__

23. A statute states: *A person who steals an article worth $1,000 or less where no aggravating circumstances accompany the act is guilty of petit larceny. If the article is worth more than $1,000, it may be grand larceny.*
If all you know is that Edward Smith stole an article worth $1,000, it may reasonably be said that

    A. Smith is guilty of petit larceny
    B. Smith is guilty of grand larceny
    C. Smith is guilty of neither petit larceny nor grand larceny
    D. precisely what charge will be placed against Smith is uncertain

23.__

Questions 24-25.

DIRECTIONS: Questions 24 and 25 are to be answered on the basis of the following section of a law.

A person who, after having been three times convicted within this state of felonies or attempts to commit felonies, or under the law of any other state, government, or country, of crimes which if committed within this state would be felonious, commits a felony, other than murder, first or second degree, or treason, within this state, shall be sentenced upon conviction of such fourth, or subsequent, offense to imprisonment in a state prison for an indeterminate term the minimum of which shall be not less than the maximum term provided for first offenders for the crime for which the individual has been convicted, but, in any event, the minimum term upon conviction for a felony as the fourth or subsequent, offense shall be not less than fifteen years, and the maximum thereof shall be his natural life.

24. Under the terms of the above law, a person must receive the increased punishment therein provided if

24.____

   A. he is convicted of a felony and has been three times previously convicted of felonies
   B. he has been three times previously convicted of felonies, regardless of the nature of his present conviction
   C. his fourth conviction is for murder, first or second degree, or treason
   D. he has previously been convicted three times of murder, first or second degree, or treason

25. Under the terms of the above law, a person convicted of a felony for which the penalty is imprisonment for a term not to exceed ten years, and who has been three times previously convicted of felonies in this state, shall be sentenced to a term, the MINIMUM of which shall be

25.____

   A. 10 years
   C. indeterminate
   B. 15 years
   D. his natural life

KEY (CORRECT ANSWERS)

1.	C		11.	A
2.	B		12.	B
3.	D		13.	A
4.	A		14.	B
5.	C		15.	B
6.	D		16.	B
7.	A		17.	C
8.	D		18.	D
9.	C		19.	C
10.	B		20.	A

21. D
22. C
23. D
24. A
25. B

PREPARING WRITTEN MATERIAL

PARAGRAPH REARRANGEMENT
COMMENTARY

The sentences which follow are in scrambled order. You are to rearrange them in proper order and indicate the letter choice containing the correct answer at the space at the right.

Each group of sentences in this section is actually a paragraph presented in scrambled order. Each sentence in the group has a place in that paragraph; no sentence is to be left out. You are to read each group of sentences and decide upon the best order in which to put the sentences so as to form as well-organized paragraph.

The questions in this section measure the ability to solve a problem when all the facts relevant to its solution are not given.

More specifically, certain positions of responsibility and authority require the employee to discover connections between events sometimes, apparently, unrelated. In order to do this, the employee will find it necessary to correctly infer that unspecified events have probably occurred or are likely to occur. This ability becomes especially important when action must be taken on incomplete information.

Accordingly, these questions require competitors to choose among several suggested alternatives, each of which presents a different sequential arrangement of the events. Competitors must choose the MOST logical of the suggested sequences.

In order to do so, they may be required to draw on general knowledge to infer missing concepts or events that are essential to sequencing the given events. Competitors should be careful to infer only what is essential to the sequence. The plausibility of the wrong alternatives will always require the inclusion of unlikely events or of additional chains of events which are NOT essential to sequencing the given events.

It's very important to remember that you are looking for the best of the four possible choices, and that the best choice of all may not even be one of the answers you're given to choose from.

There is no one right way to these problems. Many people have found it helpful to first write out the order of the sentences, as they would have arranged them, on their scrap paper before looking at the possible answers. If their optimum answer is there, this can save them some time. If it isn't, this method can still give insight into solving the problem. Others find it most helpful to just go through each of the possible choices, contrasting each as they go along. You should use whatever method feels comfortable, and works, for you.

While most of these types of questions are not that difficult, we've added a higher percentage of the difficult type, just to give you more practice. Usually there are only one or two questions on this section that contain such subtle distinctions that you're unable to answer confidently, and you then may find yourself stuck deciding between two possible choices, neither of which you're sure about.

EXAMINATION SECTION
TEST 1

DIRECTIONS: Each question consists of several sentences which can be arranged in a logical sequence. For each question, select the choice which places the numbered sentences in the MOST logical sequence. *PRINT THE LETTER OF THE CORRECT ANSWER IN THE SPACE AT THE RIGHT.*

1.   I.   A body was found in the woods.
      II.   A man proclaimed innocence.
     III.   The owner of a gun was located.
    IV.   A gun was traced.
     V.   The owner of a gun was questioned.
    The CORRECT answer is:

    A. IV, III, V, II, I   B. II, I, IV, III, V
    C. I, IV, III, V, II   D. I, III, V, II, IV
    E. I, II, IV, III, V

1. _____

2.   I.   A man was in a hunting accident.
      II.   A man fell down a flight of steps.
     III.   A man lost his vision in one eye.
    IV.   A man broke his leg.
     V.   A man had to walk with a cane.
    The CORRECT answer is:

    A. II, IV, V, I, III   B. IV, V, I, III, II
    C. III, I, IV, V, II   D. I, III, V, II, IV
    E. I, III, II, IV, V

2. _____

3.   I.   A man is offered a new job.
      II.   A woman is offered a new job.
     III.   A man works as a waiter.
    IV.   A woman works as a waitress.
     V.   A woman gives notice.
    The CORRECT answer is:

    A. IV, II, V, III, I   B. IV, II, V, I, III
    C. II, IV, V, III, I   D. III, I, IV, II, V
    E. IV, III, II, V, I

3. _____

4.   I.   A train left the station late.
      II.   A man was late for work.
     III.   A man lost his job.
    IV.   Many people complained because the train was late.
     V.   There was a traffic jam.
    The CORRECT answer is:

    A. V, II, I, IV, III   B. V, I, IV, II, III
    C. V, I, II, IV, III   D. I, V, IV, II, III
    E. II, I, IV, V, III

4. _____

5.   I.   The burden of proof as to each issue is determined before trial and remains upon the same party throughout the trial.

   II.   The jury is at liberty to believe one witness' testimony as against a number of contradictory witnesses.

   III.   In a civil case, the party bearing the burden of proof is required to prove his contention by a fair preponderance of the evidence.

   IV.   However, it must be noted that a fair preponderance of evidence does not necessarily mean a greater number of witnesses.

   V.   The burden of proof is the burden which rests upon one of the parties to an action to persuade the trier of the facts, generally the jury, that a proposition he asserts is true.

   VI.   If the evidence is equally balanced, or if it leaves the jury in such doubt as to be unable to decide the controversy either way, judgment must be given against the party upon whom the burden of proof rests.

The CORRECT answer is:

A.   III, II, V, IV, I, VI   B.   I, II,VI,V,III,IV
C.   III, IV, V, I, II, VI   D.   V, I, III,VI, IV, II
E.   I,V, III, VI, IV, II

6.   I.   If a parent is without assets and is unemployed, he cannot be convicted of the crime of non-support of a child.

   II.   The term *sufficient ability* has been held to mean sufficient financial ability.

   III.   It does not matter if his unemployment is by choice or unavoidable circumstances.

   IV.   If he fails to take any steps at all, he may be liable to prosecution for endangering the welfare of a child.

   V.   Under the penal law, a parent is responsible for the support of his minor child only if the parent is *of* sufficient ability.

   VI.   An indigent parent may meet his obligation by borrowing money or by seeking aid under the provisions of the Social Welfare Law.

The CORRECT answer is:

A.   VI, I, V, III, II, IV   B.   I, III, V, II, IV, VI
C.   V, II, I, III, VI, IV   D.   I, VI, IV, V, II, III
E.   II, V, I, III, VI, IV

7.   I.   Consider, for example, the case of a rabble rouser who urges a group of twenty people to go out and break the windows of a nearby factory.

   II.   Therefore, the law fills the indicated gap with the crime of *inciting to riot.*

   III.   A person is considered guilty of inciting to riot when he urges ten or more persons to engage in tumultuous and violent conduct of a kind likely to create public alarm.

   IV.   However, if he has not obtained the cooperation of at least four people, he cannot be charged with unlawful assembly.

   V.   The charge of inciting to riot was added to the law to cover types of conduct which cannot be classified as either the crime of *riot* or the crime of *unlawful assembly.*

   VI.   If he acquires the acquiescence of at least four of them, he is guilty of unlawful assembly even if the project does not materialize.

The CORRECT answer is:

A. III, V, I, VI, IV, II   B. V, I, IV, VI, II, III
C. III, IV, I, V, II, VI   D. V, I, IV, VI, III, II
E. V, III, I, VI, IV, II

8.   I. If, however, the rebuttal evidence presents an issue of credibility, it is for the jury to   8.____
determine whether the presumption has, in fact, been destroyed.
    II. Once sufficient evidence to the contrary is introduced, the presumption disap-
pears from the trial.
   III. The effect of a presumption is to place the burden upon the adversary to come
forward with evidence to rebut the presumption.
   IV. When a presumption is overcome and ceases to exist in the case, the fact or
facts which gave rise to the presumption still remain.
    V. Whether a presumption has been overcome is ordinarily a question for the court.
   VI. Such information may furnish a basis for a logical inference.
The CORRECT answer is:

A. IV, VI, II, V, I, III   B. III, II, V, I, IV, VI
C. V, III, VI, IV, II, I   D. V, IV, I, II, VI, III
E. II, III, V, I, IV, VI

9.   I. An executive may answer a letter by writing his reply on the face of the letter itself   9.____
instead of having a return letter typed.
    II. This procedure is efficient because it saves the executive's time, the typist's time,
and saves office file space.
   III. Copying machines are used in small offices as well as large offices to save time
and money in making brief replies to business letters.
   IV. A copy is made on a copying machine to go into the company files, while the
original is mailed back to the sender.
The CORRECT answer is:

A. I, II, IV, III   B. I, IV, II, III
C. III, I, IV, II   D. III, IV, II, I

10.   I. Most organizations favor one of the types but always include the others to a lesser   10.____
degree.
    II. However, we can detect a definite trend toward greater use of symbolic control.
   III. We suggest that our local police agencies are today primarily utilizing material
control.
   IV. Control can be classified into three types: physical, material, and symbolic.
The CORRECT answer is:

A. IV, II, III, I   B. II, I, IV, III
C. III, IV, II, I   D. IV, I, III, II

11.   I. Project residents had first claim to this use, followed by surrounding neighborhood   11.____
children.
    II. By contrast, recreation space within the project's interior was found to be used
more often by both groups.
   III. Studies of the use of project grounds in many cities showed grounds left open for
public use were neglected and unused, both by residents and by members of the
surrounding community.

IV. Project residents had clearly laid claim to the play spaces, setting up and enforcing unwritten rules for use.

V. Each group, by experience, found their activities easily disrupted by other groups, and their claim to the use of space for recreation difficult to enforce.

The CORRECT answer is:

A. IV, V, I, II, III   B. V, II, IV, III, I
C. I, IV, III, II, V   D. III, V, II, IV, I

12.   I. They do not consider the problems correctable within the existing subsidy formula and social policy of accepting all eligible applicants regardless of social behavior and lifestyle.

II. A recent survey, however, indicated that tenants believe these problems correctable by local housing authorities and management within the existing financial formula.

III. Many of the problems and complaints concerning public housing management and design have created resentment between the tenant and the landlord.

IV. This same survey indicated that administrators and managers do not agree with the tenants.

The CORRECT answer is:

A. II, I, III, IV   B. I, III, IV, II
C. III, II, IV, I   D. IV, II, I, III

13.   I. In single-family residences, there is usually enough distance between tenants to prevent occupants from annoying one another.

II. For example, a certain small percentage of tenant families has one or more members addicted to alcohol.

III. While managers believe in the right of individuals to live as they choose, the manager becomes concerned when the pattern of living jeopardizes others' rights.

IV. Still others turn night into day, staging lusty entertainments which carry on into the hours when most tenants are trying to sleep.

V. In apartment buildings, however, tenants live so closely together that any misbehavior can result in unpleasant living conditions.

VI. Other families engage in violent argument.

The CORRECT answer is:

A. III, II, V, IV, VI, I   B. I, V, II, VI, IV, III
C. II, V, IV, I, III, VI   D. IV, II, V, VI, III, I

14.   I. Congress made the commitment explicit in the Housing Act of 1949, establishing as a national goal the realization of *a decent home and suitable environment for every American family.*

II. The result has been that the goal of decent home and suitable environment is still as far distant as ever for the disadvantaged urban family.

III. In spite of this action by Congress, federal housing programs have continued to be fragmented and grossly underfunded.

IV. The passage of the National Housing Act signalled a new federal commitment to provide housing for the nation's citizens.

The CORRECT answer is:

A. I, IV, III, II   B. IV, I, III, II
C. IV, I, II, III   D. II, IV, I, III

15. I.   The greater expense does not necessarily involve *exploitation,* but it is often per-   15.____
          ceived as exploitative and unfair by those who are aware of the price differences
          involved, but unaware of operating costs.
     II. Ghetto residents believe they are *exploited* by local merchants, and evidence
          substantiates some of these beliefs.
     III. However, stores in low-income areas were more likely to be small independents,
          which could not achieve the economies available to supermarket chains and
          were, therefore, more likely to charge higher prices, and the customers were
          more likely to buy smaller-sized packages which are more expensive per unit of
          measure.
     IV. A study conducted in one city showed that distinctly higher prices were charged
          for goods sold in ghetto stores than in other areas.
     The CORRECT answer is:

     A. IV, II, I, III   B. IV, I, III, II
     C. II, IV, III, I   D. II, III, IV, I

KEY (CORRECT ANSWERS)

1.	C		6.	C
2.	E		7.	A
3.	B		8.	B
4.	D		9.	C
5.	D		10.	D

11.	D
12.	C
13.	B
14.	B
15.	C

PREPARING WRITTEN MATERIAL

EXAMINATION SECTION
TEST 1

DIRECTIONS: The sentences numbered 1 to 10 deal with some phase of police activity. They may be classified most appropriately under one of the following four categories:

    A. *Faulty* because of incorrect grammar
    B. *Faulty* because of incorrect punctuation
    C. *Faulty* because of incorrect use of a word
    D. *Correct*

Examine each sentence carefully. Then, in the correspondingly numbered space on the right, print the capital letter preceding the option which is the best of the four suggested above.

(All incorrect sentences contain only one type of error. Consider a sentence correct if it contains none of the types of errors mentioned, even though there may be other correct ways of expressing the same thought.)

1. The Department Medal of Honor is awarded to a member of the Police Force who distinguishes himself inconspicuously in the line of police duty by the performance of an act of gallantry.   1._____

2. Members of the Detective Division are charged with: the prevention of crime, the detection and arrest of criminals, and the recovery of lost or stolen property.   2._____

3. Detectives are selected from the uniformed patrol forces after they have indicated by conduct, aptitude, and performance that they are qualified for the more intricate duties of a detective.   3._____

4. The patrolman, pursuing his assailant, exchanged shots with the gunman and immortally wounded him as he fled into a nearby building.   4._____

5. The members of the Traffic Division has to enforce the Vehicle and Traffic Law, the Traffic Regulations, and ordinances relating to vehicular and pedestrian traffic.   5._____

6. After firing a shot at the gunman, the crowd dispersed from the patrolman's line of fire.   6._____

7. The efficiency of the Missing Persons Bureau is maintained with a maximum of public personnel due to the specialized training given to its members.   7._____

8. Records of persons arrested for violations of Vehicle and Traffic Regulations are transmitted upon request to precincts, courts and other authorized agencies.   8._____

9. The arresting officer done all he could to subdue the perpetrator without physically injuring him.   9._____

10. The Deputy Commissioner is authorized to exercise all of the powers and duties of the Police Commissioner in the latter's absence.   10._____

KEY (CORRECT ANSWERS)

1.	C		6.	A
2.	B		7.	C
3.	D		8.	D
4.	C		9.	A
5.	A		10.	D

TEST 2

DIRECTIONS: Questions 1 through 4 consist of sentences concerning criminal law. Some of the sentences contain errors in English grammar or usage, punctuation, spelling or capitalization. (A sentence does not contain an error simply because it could be written in a different manner.)

Choose answer
    A.   if the sentence contains an error in English grammar or usage
    B.   if the sentence contains an error in punctuation
    C.   if the sentence contains an error in spelling or capitalization
    D.   if the sentence does not contain any errors

1. The severity of the sentence prescribed by contemporary statutes - including both the former and the revised New York Penal Laws - do not depend on what crime was intended by the offender.

    1._____

2. It is generally recognized that two defects in the early law of attempt played a part in the birth of burglary: (1) immunity from prosecution for conduct short of the last act before completion of the crime, and (2) the relatively minor penalty imposed for an attempt (it being a common law misdemeanor) vis-a-vis the completed offense.

    2._____

3. The first sentence of the statute is applicable to employees who enter their place of employment, invited guests, and all other persons who have an express or implied license or privilege to enter the premises.

    3._____

4. Contemporary criminal codes in the United States generally divide burglary into various degrees, differentiating the categories according to place, time and other attendent circumstances.

    4._____

———

KEY (CORRECT ANSWERS)

1. A
2. D
3. D
4. C

———

TEST 3

DIRECTIONS: For each of the sentences numbered 1 through 10, select from the options given below the *MOST* applicable choice, and print the letter of the correct answer in the space at the right.
   A. The sentence is correct
   B. The sentence contains a spelling error only
   C. The sentence contains an English grammar error only
   D. The sentence contains *both* a spelling error and an English grammar error

1. Every person in the group is going to do his share.   1.____

2. The man who we selected is new to this University.   2.____

3. She is the older of the four secretaries on the two staffs that are to be combined. 3.____

4. The decision has to be made between him and I.   4.____

5. One of the volunteers are too young for this complecated task, don't you think?   5.____

6. I think your idea is splindid and it will improve this report considerably.   6.____

7. Do you think this is an exagerated account of the behavior you and me observed this 7.____
   morning?

8. Our supervisor has a clear idea of excelence.   8.____

9. How many occurences were verified by the observers?   9.____

10. We must complete the typing of the draft of the questionaire by noon tomorrow.   10.____

KEY (CORRECT ANSWERS)

1.	A		6.	B
2.	C		7.	D
3.	C		8.	B
4.	C		9.	B
5.	D		10.	B

———

TEST 4

DIRECTIONS: Questions 1 through 3 are based on the following paragraph, which consists of three numbered sentences.

Edit each sentence to insure clarity of meaning and correctness of grammar without substantially changing the meaning of the sentence.

Examine each sentence and then select the option which changes the sentence to express *BEST* the thought of the sentence.

(1) Unquestionably, a knowledge of business and finance is a good advantage to audit committee members but not essential to all members. (2) Other factors also carry weight; for example, at least one member must have the ability to preside over meetings and to discuss things along constructive lines. (3) In the same way, such factors as the amount of time a member can be able to devote to duties or his rating on the score of motivation, inquisitiveness, persistence, and disposition towards critical analysis are important.

1. In the first sentence, the word   1.____

   A.   "good" should be changed to "distinct"
   B.   "good" should be omitted
   C.   "and" should be changed to "or"
   D.   "are" should be inserted between the words "but" and "not"

2. In the second sentence, the   2.____

   A.   word "factors" should be changed to "things"
   B.   words "preside over" should be changed to "lead at"
   C.   phrase "discuss things" should be changed to "direct the discussion"
   D.   word "constructive" should be changed to "noteworthy"

3. In the third sentence, the   3.____

   A.   word "amount" should be changed to "period"
   B.   words "amount of" should be changed to "length of"
   C.   word "can" should be changed to "will"
   D.   word "same" should be changed to "similar"

———————

KEY (CORRECT ANSWERS)

1. A
2. C
3. C

TEST 5

DIRECTIONS: Each question or incomplete statement is followed by several suggested answers or completions. Select the one that *BEST* answers the question or completes the statement. Print the letter of the correct answer in the space at the right.

1. Of the following, the *MOST* acceptable close of a business letter would usually be: 1.____

   A. Cordially yours,   B. Respectfully Yours,
   C. Sincerely Yours,   D. Yours very truly,

2. When writing official correspondence to members of the armed forces, their titles should   2.____
   be used

   A. both on the envelope and in the inside address
   B. in the inside address, but not on the envelope
   C. neither on the envelope nor in the inside address
   D. on the envelope but not in the inside address

3. Which one of the following is the *LEAST* important advantage of putting the subject of a   3.____
   letter in the heading to the right of the address? It

   A. makes filing of the copy easier
   B. makes more space available in the body of the letter
   C. simplifies distribution of letters
   D. simplifies determination of the subject of the letter.

4. Generally, when writing a letter, the use of precise words and concise sentences is   4.____

   A. *good,* because less time will be required to write the letter
   B. *bad,* because it is most likely that the reader will think the letter is unimportant and
      will not respond favorably
   C. *good,* because it is likely that your desired meaning will be conveyed to the reader
   D. *bad,* because your letter will be too brief to provide adequate information

5. Of the following, it is *MOST* appropriate to use a form letter when it is necessary to   5.____
   answer *many*

   A. requests or inquiries from a single individual
   B. follow-up letters from individuals requesting additional information
   C. requests or inquiries about a single subject
   D. complaints from individuals that they have been unable to obtain various types of
      information

KEY (CORRECT ANSWERS)

1. D
2. A
3. B
4. C
5. C

———

TEST 6

DIRECTIONS: Each question or incomplete statement is followed by several suggested answers or completions. Select the one that *BEST* answers the question or completes the statement. Print the letter of the correct answer in the space at the right

1. The one of the following sentences which is *LEAST* acceptable from the viewpoint of correct usage is:

    1._____

    A. The police thought the fugitive to be him.
    B. The criminals set a trap for whoever would fall into it.
    C. It is ten years ago since the fugitive fled from the city.
    D. The lecturer argued that criminals are usually cowards.
    E. The police removed four bucketfuls of earth from the scene of the crime.

2. The one of the following sentences which is *LEAST* acceptable from the viewpoint of correct usage is:

    2._____

    A. The patrolman scrutinized the report with great care.
    B. Approaching the victim of the assault, two bruises were noticed by the patrolman.
    C. As soon as I had broken down the door, I stepped into the room.
    D. I observed the accused loitering near the building, which was closed at the time.
    E. The storekeeper complained that his neighbor was guilty of violating a local ordinance.

3. The one of the following sentences which is *LEAST* acceptable from the viewpoint of correct usage is:

    3._____

    A. I realized immediately that he intended to assault the woman, so I disarmed him.
    B. It was apparent that Mr. Smith's explanation contained many inconsistencies.
    C. Despite the slippery condition of the street, he managed to stop the vehicle before injuring the child.
    D. Not a single one of them wish, despite the damage to property, to make a formal complaint.
    E. The body was found lying on the floor.

KEY (CORRECT ANSWERS)

1. C
2. B
3. D

———

REPORT WRITING

EXAMINATION SECTION
TEST 1

DIRECTIONS: Each question or incomplete statement is followed by several suggested answers or completions. Select the one that BEST answers the question or completes the statement. *PRINT THE LETTER OF THE CORRECT ANSWER IN THE SPACE AT THE RIGHT.*

Questions 1-5.

DIRECTIONS: Questions 1 through 5 are to be answered on the basis of the following sample of a report relating to a civilian complaint against a member of the force. The sample report consists of fourteen numbered sentences, some of which may not be consistent with the principles of good police report writing.

1. The undersigned responded to the resident apartment of the complainant, Mrs. Eve Black, a female, 30 years of age, of 286 6th Avenue, apartment 4D. 2. Mrs. Black alleged that Police Officer M, shield #728, used abusive language to her while she was interceding on behalf of her son, Matt Black, M/W/10, same address, who was being reprimanded by the police officer for playing on the grass in front of 286 6th Avenue. 3. Response to this incident by the undersigned was as a result of a notification received from the Desk Officer, Lieutenant A. 4. Mrs. Black went on to say that the police officer stated to her, "Mind your own damn business, or I'll lock you up." 5. Complainant advised that there were three witnesses to the alleged remark - her son and two adult females, identities and addresses unknown. 6. The undersigned was unable to find and interview the alleged female witnesses. 7. Matt Black, when interviewed, corroborated his aunt's version of the incident. 8. Interviewed Police Officer M, who stated that he was in fact involved in an incident with the complainant, and he prepared a memorandum book entry in connection therewith. 9. The undersigned reviewed the entry concerned. 10. Police Officer M stated that, at the time and place of occurrence, while reprimanding a youth, then the youth's mother became enraged and threatened to "get the officer's job." 11. The officer denied the allegation of use of abusive language and further advised that there were no witnesses present. 12. He stated that at the time in question his radio was not operating properly. 13. It is apparent from the information obtained during this investigation that Mrs. Black's allegation is without substance, and that she dislikes Police Officer M as a result of previous contacts with him. 14. It is recommended that this matter be filed without prejudice to the officer concerned.

1. Which of the following sentences does NOT appear in its proper sequence in the report?   1.____

    A. 3   B. 5   C. 9   D. 11

2. Which one of the following sentences contains material which is LEAST relevant to this report?   2.____

    A. 2   B. 4   C. 10   ,   D. 12

3. Which one of the following important aspects of report writing was omitted from this report?   3.____

    A. Where   B. What   C. Who   D. When

4. Which one of the following sentences from the report contains material which apparently CONTRADICTS other information given in the report?

   A. 7   B. 8   C. 9   D. 10

4.___

5. Which one of the following sentences from the sample report contains a conclusion which is NOT based on facts provided in the report?

   A. 1   B. 3   C. 4   D. 13

5.___

Questions 6-8.

DIRECTIONS: Questions 6 through 8 are to be answered on the basis of the following report relating to a community relations police officer under your command. The report consists of ten numbered sentences which may or may not be correct or consistent with principles of good report writing.

1. Mrs. Dorothy Lew of 7686 E. Elm Street started the meeting by complaining that neighborhood children continually loiter on the sidewalk in front of her residence, annoying residents of her building. 2. The undersigned was directed to attend a meeting of community residents by the Captain. 3. The meeting, scheduled to start at 1830 hours, actually began at 1915 hours. 4. Present at the meeting were Sergeant Joseph Patt of the Youth Division, Mr. Fred Price, head of a local merchant's group, Ms. Susan May, president of the community group, several residents of the neighborhood, and the undersigned. 5. Mr. Jeffrey Brown, of 7688 E. Elm Street, stated that conditions in front of the building at which he resides had improved since the last meeting. 6. Mrs. Mary Pence, of 7690 E. Elm Street, complained that vandalism in her building was still a serious problem. 7. Mrs. Pence added that the County had not yet lived up to the promises made to the tenants. 8. Mrs. Maria Garcia stated that mailbox tampering and vandalism continued to be a problem in her building, 7692 E. Elm Street. 9. The undersigned, when called upon to speak, told the group that special attention would be given to premises 7688, 7690, and 7692 E. Elm Street in an effort to alleviate the conditions reported. 10. The meeting concluded at 2100 hours.

6. Of the following, the MOST logical sequence for the first four sentences of the report is

   A. 3, 2, 4, 1   B. 3, 1, 4, 2
   C. 2, 3, 4, 1   D. 4, 1, 3, 2

6.___

7. Which one of the following sentences contains material which is LEAST relevant to the report?

   A. 1   B. 2   C. 5   D. 7

7.___

8. Based on the report, the police officer concerned FAILED to respond to the complaint made by

   A. Lew   B. Brown   C. Pence   D. Garcia

8.___

Questions 9-11.

DIRECTIONS: Questions 9 through 11 are to be answered on the basis of the following portion of an Unusual Occurrence Report consisting of sixteen numbered sentences, some of which may not follow the principles of good report writing. Assume that one of your subordinates has submitted this report to you for your review, and that all necessary control numbers have been properly assigned and included.

1. On June 17, at about 1520 hours, Officer Chou, while on routine patrol, was approached by an apparently distraught female who stated to the officer that a male presently on the street had raped her on a previous occasion. 2. The officer, accompanied by the female, responded to the location where she pointed to a male as the perpetrator. 3. The officer noted that the male was wearing a dark jacket. 4. As the officer approached, the rapist turned and fled. 5. As the officer gave pursuit, he notified his command via radio, requesting that other units be notified of the pursuit in progress. 6. The officer was joined by two other officers in their pursuit. 7. Approximately 300 feet into the chase, the suspect fled into a building through an emergency exit and was apprehended by an officer inside. 8. The male was removed to the station house by officers. 9. A search of the street for the complainant proved fruitless. 10. At 510 hours, the male was taken to the Detective Office for further investigation. 11. At the Detective Office, the male was questioned by two detectives. 12. Determination as to the conclusion of the matter was made by the desk officer. 13. Further efforts by the desk officer to locate the complainant were negative. 14. Officer Chou was directed by the desk officer to prepare a Stop and Frisk report, 15. Officer Chou and the desk officer conferred as to the determination and he went to meal. 16. Necessary forms were prepared and forwarded as per departmental policy.

9. Which of the following sentences contains material which is CONTRADICTED by other information given in the report?　　9.____

    A. 5　　　　　　B. 6　　　　　　C. 9　　　　　　D. 10

10. Which one of the following sentences contains a conclusion which may NOT be justified?　10.____

    A. 4　　　　　　B. 8　　　　　　C. 11　　　　　　D. 14

11. Which one of the following sentences is AMBIGUOUS?　　11.____

    A. 9　　　　　　B. 14　　　　　　C. 15　　　　　　D. 16

Questions 12-14.

DIRECTIONS: Questions 12 through 14 are to be answered on the basis of the following example of a police report. The report consists of nine numbered sentences, some of which are not consistent with the principles of good police report writing.

1. At 10:30 P.M., May 23, I received a radio message from Sergeant William Smith, who directed me to report to the Tremont Motel, 10 Wilson Avenue, to investigate an attempted burglary. 2. When I arrived at the motel at 10:45 P.M., John Jones told me that he had seen a blue sedan park across the street earlier in the evening. 3. A few minutes later, Jones heard a noise at the far end of the motel. 4. Noticing that the door to one of the motel units was open, Jones walked in and saw a man about six feet tall and 25-30 years old. 5. When he saw Jones, the man ran into the next room and escaped through a window. 6. While returning to the motel office, Jones passed several cars parked in front of other units. 7. He then saw the man run across the street and get into the blue sedan, which immediately sped away. 8. No evidence was obtained at the scene of the attempted burglary. 9. Jones could not remember the license number of the car, but he thought that it was an out-of-state license plate.

12. A good police report should be arranged in logical order. Which of the following sentences from the report does NOT appear in its proper sequence in the report?

    A. 3   B. 5   C. 7   D. 9

13. Only material that is relevant to the main thought of a report should be included. Which of the following sentences from the report contains material which is LEAST relevant to this report?

    A. 2   B. 3   C. 6   D. 8

14. Police reports should include all essential information. Which of the following sentences from the report is LEAST complete in terms of providing necessary information?

    A. 2   B. 4   C. 5   D. 9

15. Suppose you have to write a report on a serious infraction of rules by one of the men you supervise. The circumstances in which the infraction occurred are quite complicated. The BEST way to organize this report would be to

    A. give all points equal emphasis throughout the report
    B. include more than one point in a paragraph only if necessary to equalize the size of paragraphs
    C. place the least important points before the most important points
    D. present each significant point in a separate paragraph

KEY (CORRECT ANSWERS)

1.	A		6.	C
2.	D		7.	D
3.	D		8.	A
4.	A		9.	D
5.	D		10.	A

11.	C
12.	D
13.	C
14.	A
15.	D

———

TEST 2

DIRECTIONS: Each question or incomplete statement is followed by several suggested answers or completions. Select the one that BEST answers the question or completes the statement. *PRINT THE LETTER OF THE CORRECT ANSWER IN THE SPACE AT THE RIGHT.*

1. All police officers wish to achieve higher rank.
   Most police officers who achieve higher rank have studied diligently.
   Some police officers who achieve higher rank have not studied at all.
   Which of the following BEST presents the above information?

   A. Diligent study by most police officers permits them to achieve higher rank but some do not study.
   B. While all police officers wish to achieve higher rank, most, but not all, study diligently to do so.
   C. Diligent study is required for most police officers who wish to achieve higher rank.
   D. In order for all police officers to achieve their wish for higher rank, most, but not all, must study to achieve it.

   1.____

2. In order to properly prepare a budget, facts are needed. These facts must be current and accurate.
   Without such facts, no budget can be prepared.
   Which of the following BEST presents the above information?

   A. Without facts which are up to date and accurate, a budget cannot be prepared.
   B. Because facts are needed to prepare a budget, they must be current and accurate.
   C. Without facts, which are needed to properly prepare a budget, no budget can be prepared.
   D. Facts are the sine qua non of budget preparation.

   2.____

Questions 3-7.

DIRECTIONS: Questions 3 through 7 are to be answered on the basis of the information given below.

   Assume that you and your partner, Police Officer Sam, have investigated the report of a terrorist threat to derail a passenger train on the Amtrak line passing through your command. Assume further that you will have to prepare a report based on the following notes:

   - Station Master, Joe Jackson, received a threat by telephone.
   - I searched the train station and tracks with Sam and Jackson; found no bomb.
   - Jackson said the caller sounded like a Japanese immigrant.
   - He reported that the caller said, *A bomb will go off in 1/2 hour on the tracks just outside the station platform,* and then hung up.
   - Jackson said that a man entered the station about a half hour before the call; he studied several booklets of train schedules.
   - He said that he asked the man where he wanted to go, and the man replied, *I want free passage to New York City.*
   - Mr. Jackson said that he replied, *There are no free passages. If you want a ticket you must pay. If you won't pay, please leave the station.*

- A bystander heard the commotion, saw the man leave, and recognized him as a chauffeur for a foreign ambassador who lives at 969 Book Street.
- We went to the address and spoke with a man who said his name was Wang Chung, and that he was a chauffeur for the Chinese Embassy.
- Mr. Chung said he had been home all day and had not been at the train station.

In each of the following questions, select the choice which MOST clearly and accurately restates the relevant information from the notes. Grammar and style are only important if they affect clarity and accuracy.

3. A. Sam, Jackson, and I searched the station and tracks, but there was no bomb.   3.____
    B. By searching the station and tracks, Sam, Jackson, and I found there was no bomb.
    C. Sam, Jackson, and I searched the station and tracks and found no bomb.
    D. After a search of the station and tracks, Sam, Jackson, and I found no bomb.

4. A. Jackson reported that the caller, a Japanese immigrant, said, *A bomb will go off in*   4.____
       1/2 hour on the tracks just outside the station platform.
    B. According to Jackson, the caller sounded like a Japanese immigrant and said, *A bomb will go off in 1/2 hour on the tracks just outside the station platform.*
    C. Jackson reported that a Japanese immigrant caller had said, *A bomb will go off in 1/2 hour on the tracks just outside the station platform.*
    D. A person who sounded like a Japanese immigrant called and said, *A bomb will go off in 1/2 hour on the tracks just outside the station platform.*

5. A. According to Jackson, he asked the man to leave the station after telling him that if   5.____
       the man would not pay he would have to leave.
    B. According to Jackson, the man didn't have the money to buy a ticket so he asked him to leave the station.
    C. Jackson said that the man refused to buy a ticket when he told him he would have to leave the station.
    D. Jackson said that the man was asked to leave the station because he could not buy a ticket.

6. A. One half hour before the call, Jackson said, a man entered the station; he said that   6.____
       the man studied several booklets of train schedules.
    B. One half hour before the call, Jackson said that a man entered the station and studied several booklets of train schedules.
    C. One half hour before police arrived, Jackson said, he received a telephone threat about a bomb.
    D. Jackson stated that 1/2 hour before he received a telephone bomb threat, a Japanese immigrant was at the station studying train schedules.

7. A. The chauffeur for the Chinese Embassy said he had been home all day.   7.____
    B. The chauffeur who lived at 969 Book Street worked for the Chinese Embassy and was at home all day.
    C. Mr. Chung, who said he was a chauffeur for the Chinese Embassy was at home all day and had not been at the train station.
    D. A man who identified himself as Wang Chung and a chauffeur for the Chinese Embassy said that he had been home all day and had not been at the station.

Questions 8-12.

DIRECTIONS: Questions 8 through 12 are to be answered on the basis of the information below.

Assume that you and your partner, Police Officer Smith, have investigated a report of an arson threat at Public School 276. You must also assume that you will be expected to prepare a report based solely on the following notes:

- The school principal, Frank Adams, received threat by telephone.
- I searched school with Smith and Adams; found no incendiary device.
- Adams said the caller sounded like a young boy.
- He reported that the caller stated, *A fire will start in the school in an hour or two.*
- Adams said that two young boys entered the school about an hour before the call; asked if the gymnasium was available to non-students on Saturdays.
- One of the boys identified himself as Jason Mason, 86 Front Street.
- We went to that location.
- Spoke with Grayson Mason, his son, Jason, son's friend, Paul Mall.
- The boys confirmed Adams' story.
- The boys also said they did not call the school.
- Grayson Mason said boys had been in his yard playing touch football; he had not heard the boys enter the house; no phone calls being made.
- There is a phone extension in Jason's room.

In each of the following questions, choose the choice which MOST clearly and accurately states the relevant information from the notes. Grammar and style are important ONLY when they impact on clarity and accuracy.

8. A. Smith and I searched the school with Mr. Adams, but there was no incendiary device.
   B. After Smith, Adams, and I searched the school, no incendiary device was found.
   C. Smith, Adams, and I searched the school, but there was no incendiary device.
   D. Neither Smith, Adams, nor I found an incendiary device when we searched the school.

8.___

9. A. Adams stated that the caller, a young boy, had said, *A fire will start in the school in an hour or two.*
   B. According to Adams, the caller sounded like a young boy and had said, *A bomb will go off in the school in an hour or two.*
   C. Adams said that the caller, who sounded like a young boy had said, *A fire will start in the school in an hour or two.*
   D. Smith said that a caller, who sounded like a young boy, had stated that, *A fire will start in the school in an hour or two.*

9.___

10. A. An hour before the call Adams stated that two young boys entered the school and asked if the gymnasium was available to non-students on Saturdays.
    B. Adams said that the two teenaged boys who had entered the school had asked if the gymnasium was available to non-students on Saturdays.
    C. Adams said that two young boys entered the school about an hour before the phone call was received and asked if the gymnasium was available to non-students on Saturdays.
    D. Two teenaged boys entered the school about an hour before the phone call was received and asked if the gymnasium was available to non-students on Saturdays.

10.____

11. A. The officers spoke with Jason Mason, his son, Grayson, and Paul Mall.
    B. The boys confirmed Adams' story, but denied making the call.
    C. Grayson Mason said that the boys did not make any phone calls.
    D. Grayson Mason stated that the boys were wrestling in the yard at the time of the phone call.

11.____

12. A. Grayson Mason said that he did not hear a phone call being made because there is a phone extension in Jason's room.
    B. Because there is a phone extension in Jason's room, Grayson Mason did not hear the phone call being made.
    C. There is a phone extension in Jason's room. Grayson Mason stated that he heard no phone calls being made.
    D. The boys confirmed everything that Mr. Adams reported.

12.____

13. Sam was clearing his driveway after a heavy snowstorm. He was clearing it in order to get to work on time.
He suffered a heart attack and died before he finished the job.
Which one of the following BEST presents the information given above?

13.____

    A. Because he was in a hurry to get to work, Sam suffered a fatal heart attack while clearing his driveway after a heavy snowstorm.
    B. Because of a heavy snowstorm, Sam suffered a heart attack in order to get to work after it.
    C. Sam, while clearing his driveway in order to get to work after a heavy snowstorm, suffered a fatal heart attack before finishing the job.
    D. Before he could finish shoveling his driveway in order to get to work after a heavy snowstorm, Sam suffered a fatal heart attack and died.

14. An auxiliary police officer named Sue was patrolling her post.
She surprised a woman trying to break into a closed liquor store.
The woman tried to hit Sue with a pinch bar.
Which of the following BEST presents the information given above?

14.____

    A. While Auxiliary Police Officer Sue was patrolling her post, she surprised a woman trying to break into a closed liquor store. The woman tried to hit her with a pinch bar.
    B. While she was patrolling her post, Auxiliary Police Officer Sue surprised a woman trying to break into a closed liquor store and she tried to hit her with a pinch bar.

C. The woman trying to break into a closed liquor store was surprised by Auxiliary Police Officer Sue who was patrolling her post and tried to hit her with a pinch bar.
D. The woman tried to hit Auxiliary Police Officer Sue, who was patrolling her area, and surprised her while she was trying to break into a closed liquor store.

15. The assigned detective returned from investigating the crime.
When he returned he gave some details to his supervisor.
The supervisor included these details in a written report.
Which of the following BEST presents the information given above?

15.

A. When he returned from investigating the crime, the detective gave some details to his supervisor, and he included this information in a written report.
B. Upon returning from investigating the crime, the supervisor included the details the detective gave him in a written report.
C. Upon his return from investigating the crime, the detective gave some details to his supervisor and then included them in a written report.
D. When he returned from investigating the crime the detective gave some details to his supervisor, who then included the details in a written report.

____

KEY (CORRECT ANSWERS)

1.	B	6.	A
2.	A	7.	D
3.	C	8.	D
4.	B	9.	C
5.	A	10.	C

11.	B
12.	C
13.	C
14.	A
15.	D

____

ANSWER SHEET

TEST NO. _____ PART _____ TITLE OF POSITION _____

(AS GIVEN IN EXAMINATION ANNOUNCEMENT - INCLUDE OPTION, IF ANY)

PLACE OF EXAMINATION _____ DATE _____

(CITY OR TOWN) (STATE)

RATING

USE THE SPECIAL PENCIL.   MAKE GLOSSY BLACK MARKS.

Make only ONE mark for each answer.   Additional and stray marks may be counted as mistakes.   In making corrections, erase errors COMPLETELY.

	A B C D E		A B C D E		A B C D E		A B C D E		A B C D E
1		26		51		76		101	
2		27		52		77		102	
3		28		53		78		103	
4		29		54		79		104	
5		30		55		80		105	
6		31		56		81		106	
7		32		57		82		107	
8		33		58		83		108	
9		34		59		84		109	
10		35		60		85		110	
11		36		61		86		111	
12		37		62		87		112	
13		38		63		88		113	
14		39		64		89		114	
15		40		65		90		115	
16		41		66		91		116	
17		42		67		92		117	
18		43		68		93		118	
19		44		69		94		119	
20		45		70		95		120	
21		46		71		96		121	
22		47		72		97		122	
23		48		73		98		123	
24		49		74		99		124	
25		50		75		100		125	

ANSWER SHEET

TEST NO. _____ PART _____ TITLE OF POSITION _____

(AS GIVEN IN EXAMINATION ANNOUNCEMENT - INCLUDE OPTION, IF ANY)

PLACE OF EXAMINATION _____ DATE _____

(CITY OR TOWN)   (STATE)

RATING

USE THE SPECIAL PENCIL. MAKE GLOSSY BLACK MARKS.

	A B C D E		A B C D E		A B C D E		A B C D E		A B C D E
1	⋮⋮⋮⋮⋮	26	⋮⋮⋮⋮⋮	51	⋮⋮⋮⋮⋮	76	⋮⋮⋮⋮⋮	101	⋮⋮⋮⋮⋮
2	⋮⋮⋮⋮⋮	27	⋮⋮⋮⋮⋮	52	⋮⋮⋮⋮⋮	77	⋮⋮⋮⋮⋮	102	⋮⋮⋮⋮⋮
3	⋮⋮⋮⋮⋮	28	⋮⋮⋮⋮⋮	53	⋮⋮⋮⋮⋮	78	⋮⋮⋮⋮⋮	103	⋮⋮⋮⋮⋮
4	⋮⋮⋮⋮⋮	29	⋮⋮⋮⋮⋮	54	⋮⋮⋮⋮⋮	79	⋮⋮⋮⋮⋮	104	⋮⋮⋮⋮⋮
5	⋮⋮⋮⋮⋮	30	⋮⋮⋮⋮⋮	55	⋮⋮⋮⋮⋮	80	⋮⋮⋮⋮⋮	105	⋮⋮⋮⋮⋮
6	⋮⋮⋮⋮⋮	31	⋮⋮⋮⋮⋮	56	⋮⋮⋮⋮⋮	81	⋮⋮⋮⋮⋮	106	⋮⋮⋮⋮⋮
7	⋮⋮⋮⋮⋮	32	⋮⋮⋮⋮⋮	57	⋮⋮⋮⋮⋮	82	⋮⋮⋮⋮⋮	107	⋮⋮⋮⋮⋮
8	⋮⋮⋮⋮⋮	33	⋮⋮⋮⋮⋮	58	⋮⋮⋮⋮⋮	83	⋮⋮⋮⋮⋮	108	⋮⋮⋮⋮⋮
9	⋮⋮⋮⋮⋮	34	⋮⋮⋮⋮⋮	59	⋮⋮⋮⋮⋮	84	⋮⋮⋮⋮⋮	109	⋮⋮⋮⋮⋮
10	⋮⋮⋮⋮⋮	35	⋮⋮⋮⋮⋮	60	⋮⋮⋮⋮⋮	85	⋮⋮⋮⋮⋮	110	⋮⋮⋮⋮⋮

Make only ONE mark for each answer.   Additional and stray marks may be
counted as mistakes.   In making corrections, erase errors COMPLETELY.

	A B C D E		A B C D E		A B C D E		A B C D E		A B C D E
11	⋮⋮⋮⋮⋮	36	⋮⋮⋮⋮⋮	61	⋮⋮⋮⋮⋮	86	⋮⋮⋮⋮⋮	111	⋮⋮⋮⋮⋮
12	⋮⋮⋮⋮⋮	37	⋮⋮⋮⋮⋮	62	⋮⋮⋮⋮⋮	87	⋮⋮⋮⋮⋮	112	⋮⋮⋮⋮⋮
13	⋮⋮⋮⋮⋮	38	⋮⋮⋮⋮⋮	63	⋮⋮⋮⋮⋮	88	⋮⋮⋮⋮⋮	113	⋮⋮⋮⋮⋮
14	⋮⋮⋮⋮⋮	39	⋮⋮⋮⋮⋮	64	⋮⋮⋮⋮⋮	89	⋮⋮⋮⋮⋮	114	⋮⋮⋮⋮⋮
15	⋮⋮⋮⋮⋮	40	⋮⋮⋮⋮⋮	65	⋮⋮⋮⋮⋮	90	⋮⋮⋮⋮⋮	115	⋮⋮⋮⋮⋮
16	⋮⋮⋮⋮⋮	41	⋮⋮⋮⋮⋮	66	⋮⋮⋮⋮⋮	91	⋮⋮⋮⋮⋮	116	⋮⋮⋮⋮⋮
17	⋮⋮⋮⋮⋮	42	⋮⋮⋮⋮⋮	67	⋮⋮⋮⋮⋮	92	⋮⋮⋮⋮⋮	117	⋮⋮⋮⋮⋮
18	⋮⋮⋮⋮⋮	43	⋮⋮⋮⋮⋮	68	⋮⋮⋮⋮⋮	93	⋮⋮⋮⋮⋮	118	⋮⋮⋮⋮⋮
19	⋮⋮⋮⋮⋮	44	⋮⋮⋮⋮⋮	69	⋮⋮⋮⋮⋮	94	⋮⋮⋮⋮⋮	119	⋮⋮⋮⋮⋮
20	⋮⋮⋮⋮⋮	45	⋮⋮⋮⋮⋮	70	⋮⋮⋮⋮⋮	95	⋮⋮⋮⋮⋮	120	⋮⋮⋮⋮⋮
21	⋮⋮⋮⋮⋮	46	⋮⋮⋮⋮⋮	71	⋮⋮⋮⋮⋮	96	⋮⋮⋮⋮⋮	121	⋮⋮⋮⋮⋮
22	⋮⋮⋮⋮⋮	47	⋮⋮⋮⋮⋮	72	⋮⋮⋮⋮⋮	97	⋮⋮⋮⋮⋮	122	⋮⋮⋮⋮⋮
23	⋮⋮⋮⋮⋮	48	⋮⋮⋮⋮⋮	73	⋮⋮⋮⋮⋮	98	⋮⋮⋮⋮⋮	123	⋮⋮⋮⋮⋮
24	⋮⋮⋮⋮⋮	49	⋮⋮⋮⋮⋮	74	⋮⋮⋮⋮⋮	99	⋮⋮⋮⋮⋮	124	⋮⋮⋮⋮⋮
25	⋮⋮⋮⋮⋮	50	⋮⋮⋮⋮⋮	75	⋮⋮⋮⋮⋮	100	⋮⋮⋮⋮⋮	125	⋮⋮⋮⋮⋮